Getting Services for your Child on the Autism Spectrum

of related interest:

Asperger's Syndrome
A Guide for Parents and Professionals
Tony Attwood
Foreword by Lorna Wing
ISBN 1 85302 577 1

Caring for a Child with Autism
A Practical Guide for Parents
Martine Ives and Nell Munro
ISBN 1 85302 996 3

Autism, Advocates, and Law Enforcement Professionals
Recognizing and Reducing Risk Situations for People with Autism Spectrum Disorders
Dennis Debbaudt
ISBN 1 85302 980 7

Access and Inclusion for Children with Autistic Spectrum Disorders
Let Me In
Matthew Hesmondhalgh and Christine Breakey
ISBN 1 85320 986 6

Enabling Communication in Children with Autism
Carol Potter and Chris Whittaker
ISBN 1 85302 956 4

Pretending to be Normal
Living with Asperger's Syndrome
Liane Holliday Willey
Foreword by Tony Attwood
ISBN 1 85302 749 9

Getting Services for your Child on the Autism Spectrum

Matthew G. Foley and DeAnn Hyatt-Foley

Foreword by Carol Gray

Jessica Kingsley Publishers
London and Philadelphia

The right of Matthew G. Foley and DeAnn Hyatt-Foley to be identified as authors of this work has been asserted by them in accordance with the Copyright, Designs and Patients Act 1988

First published in the United Kingdom in 2002
by Jessica Kingsley Publishers Ltd
116 Pentonville Road
London N1 9JB, England
and
325 Chestnut Street
Philadelphia, PA 19106, USA

www.jkp.com

Copyright © 2002 Matthew G. Foley and DeAnn Hyatt-Foley
Foreword copyright © 2002

Library of Congress Cataloging in Publication Data
A CIP catalog record for this book is available from the Library of Congress

British Library Cataloguing in Publication Data
A CIP catalogue record for this book is available from the British Library

ISBN 1 85302 991 2

Printed and Bound in Great Britain by
Athenaeum Press, Gateshead, Tyne and Wear

Contents

Dear Ryan,
Thank you for your help in writing this
book. Your incredible memory helped us
with the details of your story. We
would like to express our appreciation
for your willingness
and openness to allow us to share our
story with others. Most of all, we
appreciate your patience, your spirit,
and your courage to overcome the
challenges you face. You make us proud
every day. Love, Mom and Dad

Acknowledgements

We would both like to thank the following people for their help and support in writing this book. Thank you to Dr. Liane Holliday-Willey for giving us the big push we needed finally to write a book for parents and professionals documenting our experiences of educating a child with Asperger Syndrome; without your encouragement, this book may not have been written. To Pam Tanguay, thank you for spending time on the phone and email, discussing Asperger Syndrome, giving us tips on writing a book, and sharing your experiences raising a teenager with Nonverbal Learning Disabilities. Thank you to our close friends Rana Anderson, Mary Durheim, Tammy Stegall, Tamara Hannon and Rosalyn Lord, for taking the time to provide support and suggestions on how to improve our work.

In addition, we would like to acknowledge the difficult people who forced us to become more informed and involved in our son's education. Without them, Ryan might not be where he is today.

We have been blessed to make many friends along the way – too many to list. Many of our friends started out as Ryan's teachers and therapists. They developed a special bond with Ryan and, as a result of their commitment to him, became near and dear to our hearts. A special thank you to the West Texas elementary school staff, junior high school staff, and special education department for your hard work and dedication.

Foreword

Asperger Syndrome, defined in part by its characteristic challenges in social communication, is a disorder that ultimately teaches all who are willing to learn the very best social and communication skills. Arriving uninvited into lives of those diagnosed with the disorder and their families, and at times unexpectedly into the lives of unprepared and uninformed school professionals – Asperger Syndrome has a great deal to teach all of us about how to support and take care of one another. This relative "newcomer" to our lives provides us with situations and circumstances that can potentially divide us into private and uncomfortable camps, or unite us in a stronger social understanding. That's what this book is about.

The authors, Matt Foley and DeAnn Hyatt-Foley, describe their own story. Initially, their experience is similar to that of other parents of children with Asperger Syndrome – beginning with small concerns that are met with quick reassurances; continuing with reoccurring fears and well-intentioned but often misguided advice. Their son, Ryan, hits major developmental milestones and begins to speak early. He is also fascinated with oscillating fans, and loves to open and close cabinet doors – without any "typical toddler" interest in the contents – and turn light switches on and of. At the park, his activities absorb his interest to the exclusion of social contact with other children. The early social isolation of Asperger Syndrome can make parents feel alone in their fears and frustration – Ryan's activities translate into the emotional isolation of his parents and their anger with concerned family members.

Presenting extraordinary communication and social issues, children with Asperger Syndrome have the potential to teach others "best practice" in social and conflict resolution skills. For some, this potential is realized quickly – though admittedly it could knock forever on some doors without a response. The Foleys relentlessly gather and share information with varying results. Whereas some school professionals are fair and open-minded, others are difficult in their adherence to their own fears or resistance to learning and creativity.

Professionals who initially admit they are beginners in their understanding of Asperger Syndrome prove to be more helpful members of Ryan's team. In contrast, relationships with school professionals unwilling to acknowledge their lack of understanding are often challenged by confusion and conflict. These experiences ultimately help the Folrys develop an intangible expertise.

Accurate information arrives best in an envelope of respect – delivered to an audience with whom a relationship already exists. The Foleys discover that trust in the parent–professional relationship provides a common camp where disagreement and compromise are possible. The real foe becomes the worn out and weathered paradigms not equal to the updated social perspective that people with Asperger Syndrome require to thrive. Equipped with information and an effective system of delivery, the Foleys begin to share their knowledge in workshops and presentations. Their efforts lead to ties with people from all walks of life – all sharing a common interest and commitment to the welfare of people with Asperger Syndrome.

Framed by the backdrop of the experiences described in this book is practical information regarding the rights of students with Asperger Syndrome. The reader learns along with the authors – from the lessons drawn from libraries and laws, to those discovered in educational planning meetings and interactions with professionals. Though the Foleys live in Texas in the United States, their insights provide an internationally applicable outline of what to do with a diagnosis of Asperger Syndrome: where to go, what to look for, and how to create an effective team for a student.

As I read the story of Ryan and his parents, I could see myself in the many meetings and interactions that have defined my career through eyes other than my own. If I have ever questioned the importance of my words, how I say them, or the impact of my attitude and demeanor in my work, I never will again. Asperger Syndrome can be a mirror to our own vulnerability: the uncertainty of being in a situation and not knowing the answer, or admitting the answer may not currently be within reach. This book demonstrates that by standing tall in front of that mirror, and responding with honesty, trust, and a willingness to learn, we all reflect our best social self and discover new social solutions.

– Carol Gray

Preface

Several years ago we decided that we needed to write a book about our experiences in getting services for our son, Ryan. We wanted to share them with other families in the disability community, in the hope that they might benefit from knowing what we had experienced and what we had learned. We had worked with the education system and state agencies to acquire the support and services we felt Ryan needed to become a successful individual, and so our skills and knowledge about state and federal laws increased. Along the way, we also learned about human behavior. As our self-confidence grew, we both began working with other families from all walks of life. In addition to families, we encountered professionals who work with individuals with disabilities. We discovered that most people are confused by and overwhelmed with navigating their way through the disability support community. As a result, we began developing and presenting workshops to parents and professionals about how best they could go about obtaining appropriate services for their child/student. What we discovered was that our story is not unique – many other families and professionals have struggled with similar issues. The stories we hear are surprisingly consistent. Based on these stories, we saw a need to share our experiences and how we resolved the situations we encountered.

What makes our story unique is the approach we took in dealing with the anger and frustration we felt when Ryan did not automatically get the services we felt he needed – and deserved. Early on, we began researching and reading about our rights in the system, developing strategies and tactics for dealing with difficult situations (and sometimes people), and reading books on negotiation skills while making a concerted effort to build relationships with the professionals who were working with our son. Soon we found that we had made a transition from being parents to being parent/professionals.

Each chapter begins with our story of events – starting with our attempting to find out why our son was different from other children and concluding with the present day. Each chapter ends with what we learned and what you – both parents and professionals – can do.

Along the way, we discuss the difficult moments we had with people we have encountered. The purpose of discussing these events and the people involved is to show that we, like most parents, have encountered some difficult situations. We are not embittered by these experiences; we found that these situations motivated us to learn more and to hone our skills. For every difficult person we encountered, we met many more positive and helpful people. Our focus is to show the reader how we responded to the roadblocks and difficult situations. We discuss our mistakes and our triumphs, in the hope that our experiences will help other families in their pursuit of obtaining services for their child. We also hope that professionals who read our story will see a perspective of the difficulties and the joys that families of children with special needs encounter.

Matt Foley & DeAnn Hyatt-Foley

Chapter One

Getting the Diagnosis

The beginning

On 6 May 1985, we, Matt and DeAnn Foley, became the proud parents of a son: Ryan Foley. The pediatrician assured us that although Ryan was born a month early he was not premature. DeAnn's mother had carried DeAnn and her two brothers for only eight months, so we accepted the pediatrician's assurances. Together, we brought Ryan home to begin our new life as a family.

When Ryan was about a month old, DeAnn's intuition first warned her that there was something wrong. Her brother had been diagnosed with a learning disability when he was a child, and something about Ryan reminded DeAnn of him. But when she told the pediatrician that she suspected that Ryan might have a learning disability, he reassured her that her fears were unfounded – there was nothing wrong with our infant son. She left the doctor's office feeling embarrassed about having wasted his time with her irrational fears.

The child development books that we consulted showed that Ryan had hit all the major milestones during his first year. We were also encouraged by the fact that Ryan began to speak earlier than our friends' babies of the same age. Although in some areas his progress slowed during his second year, he still seemed to be developing within normal limits. While it is certainly true that when it comes to their child, all parents have an inherent bias, we received continual affirmation from others about our own. Being well-behaved, with curly blond hair and blue eyes, he attracted the gaze of strangers, who very often commented on what a beautiful child he was. In addition to being a boost to our egos, this helped us to see Ryan as a typical child and, along with the continued reassurance from Ryan's pediatrician that all children develop at different rates, helped to calm our fears that something was wrong with him.

When Ryan was around six months old, he began to suffer from ear infections that seemed to recur on a fairly regular basis. As his ear infections continued, the doctor prescribed stronger and stronger antibiotics, and when he was eighteen months old, the doctor warned DeAnn that he would have to have tubes put into his ears if the infections continued. The doctor put him on one more round of strong antibiotics and, fortunately, Ryan did not have any further ear infections. Later we thought that his frequent and long-standing problems with ear infections had negatively affected his hearing.

As Ryan matured, he began to engage in peculiar activities. We first noticed that he was developing a fascination with fans – especially with oscillating fans. He was drawn to them and would watch the blades with a look of amazement as he turned the switch on and off. Because this activity was potentially dangerous and we had every reason to believe that Ryan would continue to manipulate any fans to which he had access, we taught him to use them safely. Ryan was occasionally taken to visit a local hardware store that sold kitchen supplies and also oscillating fans. Ryan insisted on looking at the fans every time he was there. A saleslady noticed Ryan's interest and commented that there was another little boy who liked to visit their fans, making us less embarrassed about Ryan's behavior.

Another of Ryan's favorite activities was opening and closing cabinet doors. He would do this for extended periods of time, but to our amazement not once did he ever disturb the contents of the cabinets. What was inside did not seem to interest him. Ryan also spent a lot of time flipping light switches on and off. Although he could communicate well, he seemed to talk only when he needed something. He did not engage in conversations. When he was hurt or scared, he did not seek out other people to comfort him. Noises such as dogs barking seemed literally to hurt Ryan's ears: he would cover his ears and cry whenever dogs began barking. When we went to pick Ryan up from staying with a babysitter or family member, he did not seem eager to see us. He did not seem to make any distinction between his parents and others. Neither one of us can remember Ryan ever pointing to an object or mentioning an event or even expressing an interest in engaging another person in a joint activity.

Most distressing, however, was watching Ryan at the playground in the park. He never appeared interested in playing or interacting with other children. For example, during one outing on a cool spring day at the park when Ryan was around three years old, he again isolated himself from the other children. While the other children played together, Ryan was kneeling on the ground, picking up handfuls of gravel and intently watching as the granules fell through his fingers to the ground. He repeated this activity over and over again. It was not so much that he continued playing with the gravel – we had seen many other children doing the same thing; what concerned us was the fact that the other children his age were playing together while Ryan seemed to be perfectly happy playing by himself.

Neither one of us can remember our first conversation about our emerging thoughts of something being seriously wrong with our son, but little by little it became painfully apparent that we could no longer ignore the signs. Although at the time we were unable to identify the significance of Ryan's behaviors, looking back, we can now clearly see what the pediatrician and we were missing at the time: the indicators of Asperger Syndrome.

The professionals

The meeting with the pediatrician when Ryan was a month old was just the first of many such encounters with professionals in our attempt to identify what lay behind Ryan's behavior. We continued to try to locate the source of Ryan's issues. There were times when he seemed so much like other children that we wanted to believe that what we were seeing was only our imagination.

When Ryan was about three years old, we began to look for a daycare program. At the time we were both college students working on our undergraduate degrees and living in student housing. We thought that Ryan's immature social skills and/or lack of interest in other children might have been due to his limited encounters with them. We found a daycare facility within walking distance that was highly recommended and had a director who was also a licensed psychologist. A few weeks after Ryan had started attending the daycare program, the director made an appointment to talk with us. We sat in her office for about an hour, listening to her talk about her experiences and those of her staff with Ryan. She pointed out that he was more interested in the air-conditioning condenser unit than he was in playing with the other children. The psychologist was also concerned about Ryan not being able to swing on a swing or ride a tricycle. We told her that Ryan could indeed swing and ride a tricycle, but she did not seem convinced. The director suggested that we get Ryan's hearing checked; she and the staff felt that he might have a hearing problem. Because of Ryan's earlier bout with ear infections, we had always wondered whether his hearing and possibly his language development had been affected. Thinking we were finally getting somewhere, we had Ryan's ears checked but found his hearing to be within normal limits.

A few weeks after our meeting with the director of the daycare center, it became apparent to us that we needed to remove Ryan from that environment, because he did not seem to be making any progress toward interacting socially with the other children. When Matt picked up Ryan on his last day there, one of the staff told him that she would be starting her own preschool daycare program in her home. She planned on having only a handful of children, including two of her own, attend her program. Later that evening, we discussed and agreed on sending Ryan to her home after making some inquiries into licensure, references, and suitability. Ryan excelled in this smaller setting. When this daycare worker began teaching the children their numbers and alphabet, Ryan learned these skills more quickly than the other children did. We knew we had Ryan in the right environment. However, even though Ryan was now in close proximity to the other children, we noticed that he was still not actually playing with them.

Other members of our family were now beginning to suspect that there was something different about Ryan. In a conversation with her doctor, DeAnn's mother described some of Ryan's behaviors. Her doctor suggested that Ryan might have autism. She then went out and bought a book on autism and gave it to DeAnn. During this period, we learned that a cousin of Matt's, who is a nurse, had been asked to observe Ryan during a visit. Then a friend of Matt's family wrote to him expressing the family's concerns about Ryan. At this point we viewed our family's discussions about Ryan and their communication with professionals as interference, and the ways in which our families' concerns were communicated to us made us furious. We were angry partly because of this and partly because deep down we knew that they were correct in thinking that Ryan was not a typical child. At the same time, several of our close friends and DeAnn's grandparents were telling us that they did not see anything wrong with Ryan. DeAnn remembers her grandfather angrily telling her that Ryan was fine. Friends also commented on how bright he was. We became reluctant to share our own suspicions about Ryan with our family and friends.

DeAnn finally called our local public school to talk to someone about Ryan. The person she talked to, who was with the Preschool Program for Children with Disabilities, told her that she was describing a child with some developmental gaps and assured her that he would catch up. We desperately wanted to believe that Ryan's odd behavior was just in our imagination and to believe what the professionals were telling us about Ryan because we simply were not ready to accept the alternative. Deep down, we knew that something was terribly wrong, but we held on to the hope that we were mistaken.

The label

In the spring just before Ryan turned five, our local school district informed us that it was time for 'Kindergarten Round-up'. DeAnn went to the school and sat in the cafeteria with all the other soon-to-be kindergarten moms. The principal welcomed everyone to the elementary school. Everyone in the group was given needed information, including the name of our child's kindergarten teacher, and were told that, if we wished, we could meet our child's teacher before the beginning of school. Dreading the thought of Ryan starting school, we decided that we needed to meet Ryan's teacher and inform her of our concerns; we waited until just a couple of weeks before school started to do so.

Together, we sat down with the new teacher and went over our concerns. We shared that we did not know what the problem was, only that there was a problem. We requested that the school begin testing Ryan as soon as possible. The teacher assured us that everything would be fine. We asked if Ryan could meet her and see the classroom before the first day of school, and she agreed. When we took Ryan up to his new school, he looked around, but he did not say a word. The teacher talked to him, but still he remained silent. Eventually we went home. We decided that it would be best if Ryan's daycare provider were to take him to school on the first day. We feared that he would never stay at school if either one of us dropped him off. We followed through with our plans, and the teacher reported that the first day went without a hitch. Ryan had spent most of the day close to the teacher. It appeared that because he was more familiar with her, she provided the needed comfort. A few days later we were informed that the school had begun testing Ryan.

At some point early in the school year, the school counselor began working with Ryan and communicating with us. She seemed to be the staff member who had been appointed to be the liaison between the school and the parents, and although she was kind, our experience with her would later demonstrate that she had little if any training in the area of special education. Periodically she would call and provide an update on Ryan's progress in the classroom. She told us that Ryan was not interacting with the other students and that he would lie on the floor or stare into space during class time. She also told us that the school wanted us to get an evaluation from a psychologist, and that we were responsible for paying for the visit. We were shocked that we would have to pay for this evaluation, and after further discussion the counselor told us that she had managed to get the school to agree to fund it. She gave us the name of the psychologist, and DeAnn made the appointment.

The three of us arrived at the agreed-upon time. The psychologist asked us both some questions and took copious notes. Ryan was in the room with us, playing with a toy. The psychologist then asked to see Ryan by himself. As we left the room, we could hear him crying for us. We looked at each other in the fearful knowledge that neither one of us could go in to comfort him. As painful as it was, we sat in the reception area, waiting for Ryan's sobs to subside. The psychologist soon came out and said that she would send her report to the school; she was not sure what Ryan had, but she would give him the label that she felt would benefit him the most. The appointment had lasted for less than thirty minutes. After we had waited for several days, the counselor finally called to set up an appointment to discuss the psychologist's findings.

We knew that finally we would have our answer. All of Ryan's peculiarities would be explained, and we would at last have a direction in which to head. DeAnn was sure she knew the outcome of the evaluation: the label would be learning disability – Ryan was so much like her brother.

The counselor invited us into her office. She shared her office with another individual, who was asked to leave when we arrived. The room had an adult-sized desk at one end, but the three of us sat at a round child-sized table, on very small chairs. The counselor went through the report quickly. At the end, she said that the psychologist had determined that Ryan had Pervasive Developmental Disorder Not Otherwise Specified (PDD-NOS). Almost simultaneously, we asked what that was. Her answer: autism. We sat there stunned; DeAnn began to cry as the counselor continued with her report.

The grief

We drove home in silence. At home, DeAnn started to cry again. She just knew she had done something wrong while she was pregnant – that had to explain this horrible label. Matt assured DeAnn that she had done an exemplary job of being careful during her pregnancy. DeAnn thought of a girl with whom she worked – a single mom, attending law-school, and always dating. She always seemed to be leaving her child with someone else. It was so unfair that her child was normal, and our child had autism. Anger overtook DeAnn.

The following day, DeAnn went to work, pretending that everything was fine. She told her supervisor that we were okay now, since we finally had a label, and Ryan would now be in a smaller classroom. She also called her mother and told her about the diagnosis. They talked about school. When her mom cautioned us to be careful in dealing with the school, DeAnn told her that times had changed since her brother had been in school. These people were trained, and they knew what to do for Ryan. But DeAnn could tell that her mom was skeptical, despite her assurances.

While DeAnn pretended that everything was fine, Matt became sullen and non-communicative. DeAnn wanted to talk about Ryan – Matt made it clear that he did not. At times, DeAnn would watch Ryan and think that the diagnosis had to be wrong – Ryan could not have PDD-NOS. Information on the disorder was hard to find, but the information on autism did not describe Ryan. At other times, DeAnn would become angry with the families who had normal children and watch them with resentment. As the months went by, we distanced ourselves from one another. Finally, the depression came. Neither of us realized at the time that we were both going through the 'grief process.'

At the end of Ryan's kindergarten year, we asked for an in-home trainer. In doing some research on our rights in the special education process, we had learned that in Texas the Individual Education Plan committee had to discuss in-home training. We contacted several candidates and talked with parents of children with autism to find one with whom we were comfortable. The trainer came to our home once a week and began working with both of us, helping us to come to terms with Ryan's disability. She helped us to develop coping skills and to better our parenting skills. She helped us to realize that our priorities were (1) ourselves as individuals, (2) our marriage, (3) Ryan and ourselves as a family. With her help we came to see that we had to let Ryan spend time away from us, so that we could have some respite. Most importantly, she helped us to establish a level of acceptance of our situation as a family. Looking back, we now realize and understand that this 'grief process' is normal, and all families and individuals must experience each stage in their own way.

At the time, accepting the PDD-NOS label was extremely difficult. As we began to find more information on PDD-NOS, we were able to understand Ryan's needs better. We came to realize that with the appropriate interventions, Ryan would have the opportunity to live in the community with very little assistance. Gradually, we discovered that we had some measure of control over Ryan's outcome. When we were finally able to feel as if we had some control over our own lives, we began the next step towards successfully advocating for appropriate interventions.

What we learned

We look back on the first years of Ryan's life with mixed emotions. It was an overwhelming and confusing period in our lives. At times, Ryan seemed so typical, at other times, so different. One of a parent's greatest fears is that their child will not be 'normal'. We did not want to accept that Ryan had a disability. It was at this stage in our lives that we realized that we were in the grief stage of 'denial.' We could no longer ignore the signals. We had to accept that our child was not typical. As we emerged from denial, we found ourselves in the stage of 'anger' and 'depression.' We both vacillated between these three stages for years. It was not until we were able to get needed support through counseling that we began to make the transition out of denial, anger, and depression into acceptance.

Contributing to the feeling of being overwhelmed and confused was the fact that the professionals we encountered were not knowledgeable about the characteristics of Asperger Syndrome. As a result they were unable to help us find the proper resources. Instead of saying that they were not sure, they fed our tendency to deny that our child was not typical, with the result that Ryan missed out on some necessary early interventions. We now know that we should have pressed the pediatrician for an appropriate referral. We learned that we should have insisted that the woman from the Preschool Program for Children with Disabilities see Ryan, and we should not have accepted her diagnosis of the situation over the phone.

Another important lesson was our initiation into the public school system. We went into it in a naïve and trusting frame of mind, believing that those in the school system were appropriately trained to deal with Ryan's issues. We thought that if they found limitations to their knowledge on how to work with Ryan, they would acknowledge this, and we believed that the school system would provide all the support he needed. We also thought that they would offer every service available to help Ryan – that the school district and we, as Ryan's parents, were working together toward the same outcome of providing with Ryan with the very best education possible. We soon learned that we were wrong.

During this time, we realized that we had to follow our instincts when working with Ryan. We came to understand that as a family we had to pull ourselves together, accept Ryan's issues, and push the educators to provide the appropriate services. It was a type of awakening for both us. Had we known at this time in our lives what the future held for us, we do not know whether we would have had the courage to move ahead.

What you can do

- Avoid the 'appeal to authority' syndrome – sometimes well-meaning professionals miss the indicators of a child's problem.

- Listen to and follow your own instincts.

- Pay heed to family members' and friends' concerns.

- Don't take 'no' for an answer. If the first professional's advice seems incorrect, talk to another.

- Get outside help (e.g., social worker, counselor) shortly after your child has been diagnosed; a trained professional can help families to come to terms with their situation.

- Note that in the United States, schools are required to pay for evaluations they recommend.

- The 'grief process' is normal. It consists of five stages: denial, anger, bargaining, depression, and acceptance.

- It is normal to go through the stages of the 'grief process' more than once.

- Learn as much as you can about your child's disability; it helps the parent to progress to a level of acceptance about their child's issue.

- Do research to find out which agencies are available and what services they have to offer your child.

- When you encounter barriers, do not give up.

- Do not accept a diagnosis over the telephone – meet the professional in person.

- Be honest with yourself about the information you receive.

- Remember: opinions need to be supported with facts.

- Be your child's service coordinator.

- Always keep in mind that parents are the experts.

- Take advantage of respite. Everyone needs time away from their child.

- Take care of yourself first, your relationship with your partner second, and your child third. You must keep yourself healthy in order to have what you will need to attend to your relationship. With a strong relationship, together you will be more effective in addressing your child's needs.

Chapter Two

The Early Years of Elementary School

Kindergarten – fall

That fall, the school counselor advised us that Ryan would have to be removed from the regular kindergarten classroom. She offered to take us to several different classrooms that were set up for 'children like Ryan,' and told us that we would have an Individual Education Plan (IEP) meeting to get Ryan placed in the classroom. We had absolutely no idea what an IEP meeting was, and the counselor admitted that she was not very familiar with IEPs either, although she did tell us that an IEP committee was made up of educators, the parents, and sometimes other professionals. When the counselor handed us a sheet of paper stating the date and time of Ryan's meeting, DeAnn asked whether the time of the meeting could be changed, because it would interfere with her job schedule. We were told, nicely, but firmly, that the meeting could not be rescheduled. We only learned later that, according to federal and state law, IEP meetings were to be held at a mutually agreeable time. Thus began our initiation into the IEP process.

The school counselor and DeAnn spent several days visiting kindergarten classrooms on a variety of school campuses. DeAnn finally decided on one that was relatively close to our home. The classroom she thought would best meet Ryan's needs was located in a portable building adjacent to the regular school building. There were six boys attending the class, with one teacher and a teacher's aide to instruct them. The classroom was neat and organized, with samples of the students' work displayed on the walls. DeAnn asked whether there was another child like Ryan in the classroom, and the counselor replied by pointing out one of the boys and stating that he had been diagnosed with PDD. Although it did not register at the time, we later found out that members of school staff are in fact required by law to keep a child's diagnosis confidential. DeAnn watched this boy, trying to discern any behaviors that might be similar to those that Ryan was exhibiting, and after some time it became apparent to her that he was more severely disabled than Ryan. There seemed to DeAnn to be very little that this child had in common with Ryan. According to the counselor, all that was needed to have Ryan officially placed in this particular class was to have an IEP meeting.

On the day of the IEP meeting, we arrived at the school campus and were escorted to a room where several people were sitting at a large round table. We sat next to each other, feeling uncomfortable with and separate from the rest of the group. Of the ten people there we only recognized four: the principal, Ryan's kindergarten teacher, his new teacher, and the counselor. We were meeting the others for the first time. Without any inroductions one person started taking notes as another began reading a report based on his observations of Ryan. When this person finished, another individual began to read her report. This continued until five reports had been read to the IEP committee. We were totally overwhelmed by the amount of information that was given. Most of it was new to us and used special education terms we were not familiar with. The experience left us confused and frustrated. At one point, the diagnostician stated that her evaluation of Ryan indicated that he was slightly mentally retarded (MR). Hearing this for the first time in front of complete strangers was very upsetting. We were sure that her test results were incorrect, but we did not object because, at the time, we did not know that we were in a position to do so. It was not until much later that we discovered that the diagnostician had not given Ryan the entire Intelligence Quotient (IQ) test, but had made her determination that Ryan was slightly MR based on the scores derived from only a portion of the subtests. During the meeting, the committee kept using the word 'cognitive.' DeAnn finally stopped them and asked them to explain what the term meant. Except for an occasional question for clarification or to indicate that we understood, we remained silent during the entire meeting, at the end of which, we were handed a document that we were asked to sign, and the meeting was over. Ryan would begin attending his new school on the following Monday.

As soon as we arrived home after the meeting, DeAnn called her mother to tell her how it went, and to let her know that Ryan would be receiving special education services. DeAnn's brother had received special education services, so her mother had experience of attempting to secure services for him. She remembered her mother making frequent trips to the school to talk with the principal and her brother's teachers, and several times also with the superintendent of the school district. Her mother listened quietly as DeAnn told her about all the wonderful assistance Ryan would be receiving, including more one-on-one assistance in his new classroom, as well as speech therapy and music therapy. Finally, her mother said, 'You need to be prepared to fight for everything Ryan will receive.' DeAnn told her, 'Mom, you are wrong. You are talking about your experience with the school system twenty years ago. Now teachers are better trained, and they will do what is best for Ryan.' Her mother's reply was, 'Just be prepared.' When DeAnn hung up, she felt confident that her mother was wrong.

Periodically, we would go to Ryan's school to visit his classroom. Ryan was now showing evidence of making progress. He no longer lay on the floor, but began to participate in class activities. The teacher proudly showed us his work. We could see that Ryan was learning, and we felt comfortable with our decision to have Ryan placed in this environment.

Kindergarten – spring

Shortly after the beginning of the spring kindergarten semester, we had a meeting with Ryan's teacher and the special education coordinator. The latter's role was that of administrator and advisor to the teacher on what services were available through the special education department. It became apparent to us that she also acted as the gatekeeper to the services and supports that would be made available to Ryan. They suggested that Ryan be placed in a first-grade classroom on his home school campus. They briefly described what they called the Child Management Class. Based on what the educators told us, we were receptive to the idea of visiting the classroom. The meeting was arranged, and we went to the school. We were taken to a small classroom close to the administrative offices. We stood at the doorway and viewed the room. It contained several desks facing in different directions. The teacher explained that she used a level system that involved a student's earning or losing points based on how well they behaved. A student with a low number of points had a desk facing the wall. As the student earned more points, his or her desk would gradually be turned to face the front of the classroom. We felt that this classroom was not appropriate for Ryan, and decided against having him placed there. We later learned that this class was for students diagnosed as 'Seriously Emotionally Disturbed' and that it was common practice for this school district to place children with PDD in classrooms for children with behavior problems. When we discussed our reservations about this proposed placement with Ryan's kindergarten teacher and coordinator, the coordinator told us that they did not know where else to place a child like Ryan.

Several times during that spring, DeAnn had telephone conversations with a close friend from the small town in Nebraska where she had grown up. Her friend had a son a few years older than Ryan who exhibited problem behaviors at school. She and her husband had experienced a great deal of difficulty getting their son appropriate services to address his needs in public school, and as a result they had decided to have their son placed in a private school. DeAnn's friend had heard of classes like the Child Management Classes in public schools and told her that once a child was placed in one, it was very difficult to get the child out.

DeAnn then spoke with Ryan's first kindergarten teacher, who had a daughter with a learning disability, and asked her where she recommended Ryan should be placed for first grade. The teacher enthusiastically suggested that we look at three classrooms on three different elementary school campuses. We followed her advice, and after visiting the classrooms and talking with the teachers, we chose the one we thought would be best for Ryan. All of the children in the small class we chose had some type of learning disability. At the time, we had a very good feeling about the teacher, her assistant, and the classroom environment.

A few weeks later, the coordinator called to inform us that another evaluation of Ryan was needed. We later learned that the educators thought it would be beneficial if Ryan were placed on Ritalin. They told us that we could take him to a pediatrician or a psychiatrist, and confirmed, when we asked, that the school would pay. We agreed to have Ryan evaluated by the recommended psychiatrist. DeAnn called and made the appointment.

The day of the appointment was Ryan's sixth birthday. We picked him up after school, and the three of us drove to the psychiatrist's office. After a short wait, we were escorted into his office. The psychiatrist began his interview by asking us questions about our family history. At one point, he asked us whether Ryan had been a planned pregnancy, and we told him that it was not. He then asked us whether Ryan was wanted. DeAnn remembers looking in horror at the psychiatrist. She then looked over at Ryan, who had most probably heard the question, but may not have understood its meaning. Hearing this alleged professional asking us such a question in front of our child shocked us. We steadfastly answered that Ryan was wanted and loved.

The psychiatrist then asked to speak with Ryan alone. When Ryan began to cry, as we left the room, DeAnn then explained to him that she would leave her purse in the office with him. Since she always took her purse with her, Ryan understood that we would not be leaving the office. He calmed down and agreed to stay. After about ten minutes with Ryan, the psychiatrist invited us back into his office and informed us that he confirmed Ryan's diagnosis of PDD-NOS. He handed us a sheet of paper that explained the diagnosis and briefly went over it with us. Then he recommended that Ryan be placed on Ritalin, to assist him in focusing his attention. We were skeptical about the need for medication, but we listened to the doctor's recommendation. The doctor went on to recommend counseling for Ryan on a weekly basis. This he could provide for $90 an hour in addition to medication monitoring, for a total charge $490 a month for both services.

Another IEP meeting was scheduled to review the psychiatrist's recommendations. It was during this meeting that we became aware that the educators made the recommendation for an evaluation by the psychiatrist for the purpose of having Ryan put on Ritalin. The IEP committee also discussed Ryan's placement for first grade. We insisted on having Ryan placed in the classroom that we had decided on. We believe that the IEP committee agreed because they simply had no other placement suggestions, other than the Child Management Class. The committee accepted the doctor's recommendations for Ritalin therapy and counseling. Although the IEP committee had agreed to Ryan receiving counseling services, it was not documented in the IEP paperwork who would pay, leaving us with the impression that we were responsible for paying for the counseling.

Kindergarten – summer

DeAnn talked with Ryan's pediatrician about the psychiatrist's recommendation to place Ryan on Ritalin. She gave him the copy of the psychiatrist's report and asked him whether he would consider prescribing the medication. The pediatrician agreed to speak with the psychiatrist, who informed him that only a psychiatrist was qualified to monitor Ritalin prescribed for a child with PDD and as a result the pediatrician informed us that he would neither prescribe nor monitor the medication. DeAnn then contacted her parents' doctor, who had been her doctor when she lived with her parents. When she explained the situation to him, he said that it would not be a problem for him to prescribe and monitor the medication. Unfortunately, getting Ryan to his appointments would mean driving through Dallas for 45 minutes at best.

DeAnn now began to call local counselors and psychologists in order to find someone who was experienced with PDD and was also affordable. We were optimistic because several therapists based their fee on a sliding scale. Finally, DeAnn contacted a counselor who was seeing a sixteen-year-old with PDD. The counselor asked why we were paying for a service that the IEP committee had recommended, and told DeAnn that the school district paid her for this student.

After receiving this information from the therapist about payment for related services, it became apparent to us that we needed to become more informed about the services and supports to which Ryan was entitled as a student in special education, and about who was responsible for paying for them. DeAnn spent several days making phone calls to anyone listed in the phone book who worked with families of children with disabilities, and inquired about what services a child should be receiving through the public school system. After three days of making calls, DeAnn finally found a lead. The person from Advocacy Incorporated suggested that she call a Texas Parent Training and Information (PTI) Center and gave her the phone number. It turned out that the organization had an office in our location. DeAnn immediately called this agency and received the titles of several publications on special education law. After ordering these publications, we eagerly awaited their arrival.

DeAnn was so excited about knowing where to locate education law that she went to the local university and found the law section of the library. After locating Public Law 94-142, Education of All Handicapped Children Act, she started to read, and her heart sank; she could not understand what she was reading. But she reminded herself that she had a college degree, and if she just applied herself, she would understand. After another unsuccessful attempt, she gave up and went home, thinking that maybe the manuals and literature she had ordered would be easier to understand. It took several days for the literature to arrive in the mail. As luck would have it, all the literature she had ordered arrived on the same day. DeAnn sat on the living room floor and opened each package, skimming through the contents of the booklets. She felt like crying when she was also unable to understand what she was reading in the new manuals. Her initial excitement and enthusiasm turned to frustration and a feeling of being overwhelmed.

DeAnn again contacted the PTI and made an appointment to speak with someone about the information on special education law that she had recently received. When DeAnn arrived for her appointment, the director briefly explained how the special education system worked. Next, she informed DeAnn of her parental rights in the special education process. DeAnn now had a basic understanding of the process, allowing her to research independently. She spent the summer between kindergarten and first grade looking up federal and state laws governing special education. She began placing the information she accumulated on Matt's side of the bed for him to read. The stack continued to grow, untouched for several weeks, before Matt began reading the material. But when the next school year began, the new information we had received prompted us to request an IEP meeting.

First grade

The next IEP meeting was our third, but it was the first one where we truly participated in the discussions. The federal law had just been reauthorized and renamed the Individuals with Disabilities Education Act (IDEA). Through our research, we discovered not only that parents were equal participants in the decision-making process, but also that the school was responsible for paying for services and supports the IEP committee determined were appropriate for Ryan's education. DeAnn also discovered in her research that Texas has an Autism Supplemental Page: when a child has been diagnosed with autism, the IEP committee is required to address seven additional areas: in-home training, parent training, behavior modification, student/teacher ratio, minimal unstructured day, and extended year services.

Although the supplemental page was included in the IEP paperwork for the first two IEP meetings, there had been no discussion during the meetings about how the seven areas were to be addressed. We learned that it is common practice for the educators to write up goals and objectives and the services and supports they consider appropriate to meet the needs of the student before the IEP meeting. This makes sense because it saves time during the IEP meeting. The problem for us was that we had not known that what had been written prior to the meeting was only a draft until the whole IEP committee, including us, agreed to accept them. We were beginning to understand that it was up to us to learn what we could about the special education process. We discovered that the annual goals were a list of what Ryan was expected to complete by the end of the school year. The objectives were a list of the steps it would take for Ryan to achieve the annual goals. We learned that the IEP was a legal binding document that listed what the school district would provide for Ryan, and we could hold the school accountable only for those items listed in the IEP document.

Together, we came to the next meeting with a list of requests for Ryan and the legal research to support the requests; all these were stored in a black canvas bag. We later referred to the bag as the 'black bag' after we realized that bringing information, especially legal information, proved to be very helpful in our efforts to advocate for Ryan. We also began taping the IEP meetings. We found this practice to be very helpful in several ways. Replaying the tape allowed us to absorb more fully information that we had previously found difficult to understand or had missed altogether because of the pace of the meeting and the newness of the experience. With the tape, we had a record of the meeting that could be used to remind the educators of what they had said they would provide for Ryan. (We also noticed that with the tape recorder running the educators were more polite and tended to get more businesslike!) We began to make it a habit before attending an IEP meeting to discuss what to push for in the meeting and what information we needed to take with us to support our requests. We were beginning to make the transition from naïve and trusting parents to 'warrior parents.' We felt that the IEP committee was keeping us in the dark about our rights as parents and the obligations of the public school system to meet the appropriate educational needs of our son. With our growing familiarity with educational law, we felt far more confident in making the IEP committee accountable for providing the services and supports they were legally obligated to provide to meet Ryan's individual needs.

We requested an occupational therapy evaluation, in-home training, parent training, and an individualized behavior intervention plan that did not allow school personnel to use corporal punishment or aversive techniques on Ryan. The IEP committee agreed to all our requests. After this IEP meeting, we agreed that our efforts to learn about our rights and responsibilities in the IEP process were beginning to pay off. We had uncovered information about services that, up to this time, we had been unaware of. We came to the realization that we could not afford to rely on the school to offer information about all the services and supports that Ryan was entitled to receive. This motivated us to continue to increase our level of participation in the IEP meetings and to research the special education system.

A few weeks after the meeting, we met with the occupational therapist to discuss the results of her evaluation. She informed us that based on her assessment Ryan did not need occupational therapy. We felt intuitively that she was wrong but, because we did not have evidence to the contrary, we had to accept her findings. We not only found out two years later that Ryan desperately needed the occupational therapy, we also learned that we could have requested an Independent Educational Evaluation (IEE). (If a parent disagrees with an evaluation by an employee or by someone contracted with the school district, the school district has a choice: they can take the parents to mediation, or due process hearing, or agree to pay for an outside independent evaluation by a professional agreed upon by the parents and the school district.) In the United States, there are many professionals who do not work for the school districts but are in private practice. This meant that we had the option to have someone outside the school district evaluate Ryan. A due process hearing is a formal legal proceeding. Parents may request a due process hearing if they disagree with the identification, evaluation, educational placement, or other aspects relating to their child's free appropriate public education. Ryan did not receive the benefit of early intervention in this desperately needed area because we did not have the necessary information to push for occupational therapy. It is our belief that had Ryan begun occupational therapy after his first evaluation, he would now have better handwriting.

During this time, DeAnn began meeting with other parents of children with autism as a volunteer for the PTI. She helped them to prepare for their IEP meetings by sharing information we had learned through our research and experiences with special education. We joined a local support group and developed some very close friends. The two of us found it to be very comforting to associate ourselves with people who were experiencing many of the same things that we were experiencing as parents of a special needs child. We continued to read articles and books on autism. Together, we also began attending conferences.

We were happy with the progress Ryan made in first grade. When the IEP committee met in the spring to discuss second grade, it was determined that Ryan would attend school during the summer. In the fall, he was to stay with the same teacher and several of his classmates, even though the program was being moved to another campus.

Second grade

At the beginning of the fall of Ryan's second-grade year, DeAnn attended a conference on 'Inclusion' that was recommended by the director of the PTI. She did not know what Inclusion meant or what to expect from her attendance at this conference. The speaker explained that children with disabilities needed to be with their typical peers as much as possible. He said that children with disabilities should not have to earn their right to be in the general classroom. Without the experiences of learning with typical children, children with disabilities would never learn appropriate social skills. As she listened to the presenter talk about Inclusion, DeAnn became anxious at what she was hearing. At the end of the speaker's presentation, he opened the floor for questions. DeAnn challenged the speaker about what he had said about placing special education students in classes. Up to this point, we had worked very hard to have Ryan placed in a self-contained classroom, with very positive results. This presenter was essentially saying that our efforts were misplaced, and we were denying Ryan the opportunity to learn from typical peers. DeAnn again consulted the friend who had encouraged her to attend the conference and she expressed the fact that she was still extremely angry and upset with the presenter's information. The friend suggested that DeAnn do some research on Inclusion before making up her mind.

Once again, DeAnn was on a mission and began doing research. She went to the PTI (Parent Training and Information Center) office and made copies of everything in their library about Inclusion. The more she read, the more she was persuaded that Ryan needed to be with typical peers. Since the time of his removal from his first kindergarten classroom, he had spent very little time with typical children. When Matt also read the material, he, too, was convinced of the need for Ryan to spend time with general education students. We decided to approach Ryan's teachers with our idea. In our minds, it made so much sense that we did not expect to encounter any resistance from the educators.

We requested an IEP meeting. The teacher, principal, and special education coordinator gasped at our request to place Ryan in regular classes. They argued that Ryan needed to stay in the self-contained classroom. The committee insisted that Ryan was not capable of being in a general education classroom. We also requested that an aide be on the playground with Ryan to help him to learn how to interact with the other children. The principal told us that he could not provide an aide for Ryan because if he did, he would have to provide one for the other children. This, of course, sounded ludicrous to us, but we did not know how to respond to his statement without being rude. We left the meeting even more determined that Ryan would be in the regular classroom. The special education coordinator, sensing that we would continue to push for general education placement, called and offered that the school was willing to let Ryan attend a handwriting class. DeAnn explained that Ryan had a difficult time with writing. The special education coordinator then offered a math class, which DeAnn declined. Having done additional research and having attended another conference discussing the benefits of Inclusion, we went to the school and visited several second-grade classrooms, just to see exactly what these children were able to do that Ryan was incapable of doing. We observed a science class where the children were learning about penguins, utilizing many hands-on activities. This seemed perfect for Ryan. DeAnn called the special education coordinator about the science class and requested another IEP meeting. After a long debate at the meeting, the committee finally agreed to let Ryan participate in the science class. It was a small movement, but we knew that the school staff would see how well Ryan was doing and would agree to full-day general education placement for third grade.

Once again, we began the process of visiting the school in our neighborhood and preparing for Ryan's placement at his home campus. We also requested that extended school-year services for the summer should be in a group of other typical students attending summer school and after some – rather heated – discussion, the IEP committee agreed to allow Ryan to attend summer school with his typical peers. However, the teachers continued in their attempt to dissuade us from general education classes for the following school year. They listed reason after reason why Ryan would not be able to function in the general education classroom. The third-grade teacher brought in the curriculum to show us how difficult the material would be for Ryan, but we continued to argue for his inclusion.

During the spring IEP meeting, we were informed that Ryan would not be placed at his home campus. By the end of second grade, Ryan had been moved six times and had been in seven classroom settings at one of four elementary schools in only three years. Over the Christmas break during second grade, Ryan asked us what school he would be going to the following semester. Our first response was one of sadness that our son did not enjoy the comfort and security of being a student at his neighborhood school. Our son, who had social difficulties, had been bounced around the district so many times that he felt that he did not belong anywhere. We were prepared to fight to get him in general education classes at his home school.

From the time that Ryan had been diagnosed with PDD-NOS, we continued to go to the university library and find any information we could about Ryan's disorder. DeAnn finally read the book her mother had given us on autism. What we read about

PDD-NOS and autism did not accurately describe Ryan. We had managed to convince the school to contract with outside professionals who were familiar with autism to work with Ryan. All of the professionals who worked with him stated that he was not like any child with autism they had ever worked with. Our friends' children with autism did not function at the same level as Ryan. We could see that Ryan exhibited some autistic behaviors, but we knew deep down that Ryan had something else.

In the fall of 1992, as we continued our research, Matt found an article in a journal published in England. The author was Lorna Wing, and the article was about Asperger Syndrome. When DeAnn also read it, she could not believe it: it described Ryan. Neither of us had ever heard of this disorder, so we began asking professionals in our area what they could tell us about it. At that time, even if these professionals knew of the disorder, they were unable to give us any information beyond what we had read in the Wing article. Now we had a name and some general information about a disorder that fit Ryan better. Unfortunately, there was no one to consult about how to use this information to help Ryan. We decided that we needed to have him evaluated by a professional who specialized in autism. Through our parent contacts, we had already found a psychologist in Dallas who worked primarily with children with autism. We had previously met her on a couple of occasions and felt very comfortable with her.

DeAnn continued her research on special education law and at this point discovered that the school district should have paid for the initial doctor's visit requesting Ryan to be placed on Ritalin. She also discovered that the school had failed to provide the counseling services for Ryan that had been recommended by the IEP committee and written in his current IEP. We felt that this information would give us some bargaining power when we had our next meeting with the special education director.

When we arrived at the director's office, we found that she had also invited the special education coordinator to our meeting. We began explaining that counseling, as a related service, had been written into Ryan's IEP, but a counselor had not worked with Ryan even once. Both the director and coordinator responded with concern while they thumbed through their documents. We went on to point out that we had paid for the doctor's visit to have Ryan placed on Ritalin, although the school district was obligated to pay for that service, as it had been recommended by the IEP team. We calmly asked to whom we needed to submit the bill. The director said she would take care of it. Finally, we asked about the evaluation with the specialist that had been discussed. The director informed us that she, the director, had the right to choose the professional to complete the evaluation. We agreed, but pointed out that, if we disagreed with the evaluation, we could ask for an outside independent evaluation at the school's expense, so that there would be a risk to the school of paying for two evaluations. As a result the school made an appointment with the psychologist we had recommended.

After all the tests on Ryan had been administered and the parent/teacher questionnaire filled out, we sat down with the psychologist to review the results. She informed us that Ryan was a child with average intelligence, and that she had diagnosed him with high-functioning autism. We asked her what she knew about Asperger Syndrome. She said she was somewhat familiar with it, but did not elaborate. Her evaluation report gave us the information we needed to develop an appropriate educational plan for Ryan. Shortly after the evaluation was completed, we were presented with an opportunity to work in the field of developmental disabilities and, at the same time, further our education. We decided that we would move to West Texas.

What we learned

Thinking back on this time in our lives made us realize that our initial encounters with educators and the school system defined who we were becoming as parents in the public education system. In the beginning, the school personnel easily convinced us that they were working to provide Ryan with an appropriate education. As time went on, we increasingly felt that the education system was not equipped to meet our son's individual needs appropriately. We learned that in order to ensure that our son would receive what he needed and was entitled to educationally, we had to become more involved in his education by becoming informed, proactive members of the IEP team.

When we discovered that the special education department knew – or had reason to know – that payment for services recommended by the IEP committee was the responsibility of their department; we felt betrayed and foolish, and this quickly transformed into anger. As a result, neither of us viewed the educators as our allies. We learned through our conversations with other parents that they, too, were misled.

We also became aware of the fact that, to a great extent, parents and the school system were working at cross-purposes. As parents, we had an interest in having our child receive the best education possible. The school system, on the other hand, was working within a budget and was therefore engaged in practices that put limits on the supports and services they provided, in complete disregard of their responsibilities for funding them. The IEP committee was extremely resistant to providing the supports, services, or placement outside what they were accustomed to providing. We quickly learned that our ignorance would be used against us, so we began educating ourselves about educational law. We also began to research and discover 'best practices.' Because of our research, we knew what services, supports, and placements would be most appropriate and beneficial for Ryan. We attempted to hold the IEP committee accountable through the law. Together, we knew the laws governing education, but we did not possess the skills to hold the IEP committee accountable. We became frustrated when the educators refused to do what we thought was best and appropriate for Ryan. These conflicts led to feelings of frustration between the educators and us, causing friction and an adversarial relationship between the two parties.

Because we found the IEP committee so difficult to work with, we were forced to become more informed about Ryan's disability, educational laws, and best practices. This also put us in a position to become involved with other parents and to reach out into the community for support. In many ways, the difficult position we were put in by the IEP committee encouraged us to become better advocates for Ryan. Though we suspected that Ryan had Asperger Syndrome, we could not find information on interventions; however, we began to pay heed to our instincts. We continued to learn and to push the IEP committee to provide interventions we thought were appropriate. The result was that, while we did not get the placement and all the interventions we felt Ryan needed, we did succeed in getting him some of the appropriate services and supports. We know that Ryan received much more from the public school system because of our participation than he would have otherwise.

To summarize these years, we evolved from being passive parents to being involved parents. As our self-confidence in dealing with Ryan's issues grew, our relationship with one another became stronger. In the process, we became informed advocates for our son. Our reward was that we developed the skills and knowledge that helped to prepare us for our next few years in a different, but similar, education system in West Texas.

What you can do

- Be familiar with the laws governing education in your area.
- Bring another person with you to the meetings.
- Establish a filing system.
- Obtain evaluation results *BEFORE* the meeting.
- Be familiar with the evaluation report.
- Ask all the questions you need in order to understand the evaluation fully.
- If you disagree with the evaluation results, ask for an outside evaluation or get your own.
- Research your classroom options and visit these classes.
- Be familiar with the laws governing the Least Restrictive Environment.
- Research who is responsible for paying for specific services.
- Become familiar with the agencies that advocate for children with special needs. Obtain their literature. If necessary, have the information explained to you.
- Talk with other parents.
- Attend conferences.
- Read books.
- Bring research to school meetings.
- Anticipate objections, and prepare a rebuttal.
- Take the emotion out of the meetings.

- Documents that are brought to the IEP meeting (e.g., goals and objectives) are drafts until the IEP committee has approved them.

- Bring a tape recorder to all your IEP meetings.

- There are no established time limits for IEP meetings. Do not allow the IEP committee to be rushed because of a failure to schedule enough time. Either complete the meeting or adjourn it for another day.

- Do not allow yourself to be rushed into making decisions during an IEP meeting. Slow the meeting down to a pace at which you can comprehend the information, so that you can make informed choices.

- Find and participate in a support group.

- Be aware that sometimes parents' anger is misattributed to the 'anger' stage of grief. In some cases, the anger stems instead from discovering that the school district has not fully disclosed its responsibility to the child who receives special education services.

- Make your child an individual to the educators by putting a face on the issues.

- Do not let the educators limit your child.

- Remember that you, the parent, are your child's one constant throughout the education system.

Chapter Three

Second Grade – Repeated – and Third Grade

West Texas

When DeAnn became aware of a position as an Area Development Director for the Parent Training and Information Center (PTI) where she volunteered, we discussed the possibility of moving from the Dallas/Fort Worth area to West Texas. Matt was making plans to enter graduate school at the University of North Texas in Denton at the time, but he said that, if the university in West Texas had a comparable program, he would consider making the move. We did not know anyone who lived in West Texas. We were leaving our families and our friends, in addition to taking a big risk with school and our careers.

It took some time to work up the courage, but DeAnn finally contacted the special education director at the West Texas school district and informed her that we would be moving to her school district. She explained that both of us believed very strongly in Inclusion and that we expected our eight-year-old son with autism to be placed in a general education classroom, all day. She asked the director where we needed to move in order to make sure that Ryan would be placed in a general education classroom. The special education director told DeAnn that no matter where we moved in her district, she would guarantee that our son would be placed in general education classes. DeAnn asked for a couple of recommendations, expecting that some schools may be better suited to Ryan's needs than others.

When the time came for the move, Ryan stayed with one of Matt's brothers while we drove out to West Texas to find an apartment. We arrived at the hotel at 4:00 in the morning, and after sleeping for a few hours, we began the grueling task of finding a place to live. We could not find any close to campus that we both liked and could afford and, as we looked further and further afield, we were becoming concerned. It was late afternoon, and we had not found a place to live. As we left one apartment complex we noticed another directly across the street from a park. We decided to stop. The apartment complex had one last two-bedroom apartment available; we liked what we saw, so we paid the deposit. As we were leaving the complex, we noticed an elementary school a block away and wrote down the name of the school.

A few days after our trip to West Texas, the psychologist sent us the evaluation report. DeAnn called the special education director, this time telling her our names and that we had rented an apartment close to an elementary school. When DeAnn inquired about the principal, she was told that he was a 'straight shooter' and a very competent administrator. In essence, we had stumbled across an excellent school.

Six weeks later, with all our possessions ready for transport, we said our good-byes to family and friends and with Matt's brother we headed to our new home. As the three of us began hauling boxes and furniture up to the second-floor apartment, several men, who were at the swimming pool located within a few yards from our apartment door with their families, walked over to the truck, introduced themselves, and offered to help us to move in. In under an hour, everything was out of the vehicles and in our apartment. The men invited us to a cookout they were having with their families at the pool. Their generosity made us feel very comfortable in our new home.

School would be starting in two weeks, so DeAnn made an appointment with the principal. It was a hot West Texas day in the month of August. You could see the heat rising from the sidewalks and streets. As DeAnn and Ryan approached the front of the building on their short walk to the elementary school, she saw a man in a white long-sleeved shirt and tie watering the plants. DeAnn recognized that he must be the principal; she introduced herself and Ryan. The principal took them on a tour of the building. During their walk, the principal expressed his concerns about having students with special needs in a general education classroom for the entire day. He thought that these students should be provided with additional assistance in the content mastery room. DeAnn acknowledged his concerns but remained firm on our decision to have Ryan placed in a general education class all day. At about this time, they came upon a couple of students who were helping to prepare classrooms for the coming school year. The principal introduced Ryan as a new student to their campus. Although the principal had disagreed with DeAnn on a fundamental teaching issue, she walked away from the campus with a very good feeling about him.

During the latter part of the summer Matt worked on getting admitted into graduate school, while DeAnn spent her time getting to know the key people in special education. She met with the associate psychologist who would be working with Ryan and also the special education coordinator for special education services. She shared with them Ryan's academic history and discussed having an Individual Education Plan (IEP) meeting right away, to get the appropriate services and supports in place for Ryan.

As we did not have anyone to watch Ryan during the IEP meeting, we decided that DeAnn would attend, while Matt stayed at home with Ryan. DeAnn entered the school with her 'black bag' containing research and a tape recorder. She had already met most of the people in the room. She made it clear to everyone straight away that she was well acquainted with special education law and with her rights as a parent. We had decided that Ryan should repeat second grade in order to focus on social skills development without having to be concerned with academics. Ryan had demonstrated the capacity to learn in a small group setting, but he had had little opportunity to interact with typical peers. Our previous efforts to get him into general education classes had been met with strong opposition. Though retaining Ryan was not a requirement for Ryan to attend general education classes, the suggestion made our idea more palatable to the school staff. Retaining him would accomplish two goals. First, in this new school district Ryan would begin attending a general education class, where he would spend his entire day. The second goal was to have Ryan experience what it feels like to be a member of a class on only one campus for the entire school year. He would be given the opportunity to develop his social skills with typical peers. We thought he would do better socially with younger children. Ryan's new second-grade teacher was at the meeting. After much discussion, the IEP committee agreed to have Ryan placed in the general education classroom for the entire day, with no pullouts. Ryan's new teacher and the principal expressed their reservations about having a special needs child in a general education classroom all day, but they agreed to give it a try. The IEP committee also agreed that school staff would provide in-home training, parent training, and speech therapy. DeAnn left the IEP feeling elated.

Second grade, repeated – fall

DeAnn took Ryan to the elementary school on the first day of classes. In the past, the school bus had always taken Ryan to school, so she was excited about walking Ryan to school and dropping him off at his classroom, just like other parents. When DeAnn and Ryan arrived at the classroom door, Ryan's new teacher greeted them. DeAnn introduced Ryan, and the first thing Ryan said to her was that his favorite color was blue. DeAnn could tell that Ryan was comfortable with his new teacher. After showing Ryan to his seat, the teacher told DeAnn that although she had never worked with a child like Ryan, she was looking forward to the opportunity.

It was encouraging that Ryan seemed comfortable with his new teacher, but this was not enough to keep us from worrying about how he was doing at school. When it was time to pick him up, DeAnn arrived early and stood in the hallway outside Ryan's classroom, along with several other parents. When the dismissal bell rang, Ryan emerged from his classroom and seemed to be okay. When DeAnn asked his teacher how his day had gone, she said Ryan did just fine.

Standing out in the hall and talking with the teacher every day became a five-year ritual. It allowed us to check with the teachers about how Ryan was doing, and it gave them the opportunity to voice any concerns. Another advantage of taking Ryan to school and picking him up was the friendships we made with some of the parents who waited in the hallway with us. One man who waited for his children was from New Zealand. Our families became good friends as a result of our hall time.

Early into the school year, Ryan began to chew on the collar of his shirts. He came home with his shirts looking like Swiss cheese. After talking to his teacher, we agreed with her that his chewing his shirts was probably a reaction to feeling stressed at school. Fortunately, the shirt chewing lasted for only a few weeks, and other than this, we were not able to detect any signs that suggested that Ryan was experiencing undue stress. By all accounts, he seemed to be handling his new education setting just fine. We noticed that several of his classmates began talking and playing with Ryan. We were both extremely happy about the prospect of Ryan making friends.

Moving to a new town meant finding another pediatrician for Ryan. DeAnn began talking with parents whom she was assisting with educational matters, to get recommendations for a good pediatrician. One day a mother excitedly told her about a pediatrician who had just started his own practice. She went on to state that he was accepting new patients, but his practice was filling up quickly. DeAnn made an appointment and brought information about high functioning autism to the meeting for the doctor to read; she explained Ryan's specific issues to him. DeAnn felt very comfortable with him, and he seemed truly interested in working with a child like Ryan – he has been Ryan's pediatrician ever since. He demonstrated his interest by reading the information on autism that DeAnn gave him, and he would always ask about how Ryan was doing in school. He would also refer parents of special needs children to us when they had questions about the special education process or how to get services. When the pediatrician had interns working in his office and he had an appointment with Ryan, he provided the interns with the opportunity to talk with them. We feel that it is very important that current and future medical professionals become acquainted with children like our son in order to motivate them to learn more about the disorder. Had Ryan's first pediatrician been aware of the characteristics of Asperger Syndrome, Ryan could have had some much-needed early intervention.

In addition to graduate school, Matt had been accepted into a program that taught individuals with disabilities and parents of children with disabilities how to advocate for their rights on a local and state level. He would spend one weekend a month for eight months traveling to Austin. Each time, he would come back with new information that reinforced our belief in Inclusion.

Ryan made progress socially during the course of the school year, although he continued to want to talk only about his special interests. The speech therapist offered to start an after-school therapy session for Ryan that would include other children. She found three students in Ryan's class who, she felt, would be good role models for Ryan. We told her that she should inform the parents that we would be happy to transport their children home after the session. When she contacted the parents, they all agreed to let their children participate. The kids named their group 'The Fun Club.' The therapist came up with various activities for the students that promoted social interaction. Ryan began looking forward to this special time with his 'circle of friends.'

DeAnn had made it a habit to call the special education director from time to time to talk with her about how Ryan was progressing. During one conversation, DeAnn commented that Ryan hated to dry off with a towel after taking a shower; she also told her about how fussy he was about wearing certain kinds of clothing and how very particular he was about the foods he would eat. The special education director responded that it sounded as if Ryan may be tactilely defensive; he needed to undergo a sensory integration (SI) evaluation. Although she had no idea what that was, DeAnn made arrangements for the evaluation. An occupational therapist assessed Ryan and determined that he did indeed need SI therapy. As we did not want Ryan pulled out of class for this service, we made arrangements for him to go to her office once a week after school for SI therapy, in addition to occupational therapy. DeAnn remembers watching the first few sessions and thinking that all the occupational therapist and Ryan were doing was playing games. She did not understand how playing games would benefit Ryan, but she continued to take him to the therapy sessions. Within several weeks of the beginning of SI therapy, we noticed some changes. Ryan's coordination was improving, and he was beginning to tolerate wearing clothing that in the past we could not get him to wear. He also became more receptive to trying new foods. This was especially encouraging because he would eat a limited variety of foods, and we were concerned that his nutritional needs were not being met. We were amazed by the changes taking place as a result of SI therapy and became firm believers in the need for continuing this therapy.

Second grade – spring

In early spring, when Ryan came home from school, he would tell us about a boy in his class who was telling dirty jokes and using profanity. What concerned us more was that this boy was picking on Ryan. When we talked to Ryan's teacher and the school principal, they told us that they were aware of the problem. We learned from other parents that this child had a history of exhibiting these types of behaviors. Ryan continued to come home with stories and colorful words and statements. One night, when DeAnn was taking members of the 'The Fun Club' home, she noticed that Ryan was talking to the other children about this child. One of them turned to Ryan and said, 'Don't feel bad, Ryan, he does that to everyone.' When she heard those words of encouragement, DeAnn realized that the friendships that were developing also provided a support system for Ryan. Fortunately for Ryan and his classmates, the child with behavior problems moved at the end of the school year.

As the Area Development Director for the PTI, DeAnn would occasionally attend the IEP meetings of other parents. This provided her with a wealth of information without the emotional burden that parents have to deal with at their own child's IEP meetings. She also attended conferences and workshops on special education law. Inclusion was the hot topic that year, so she would hear someone speak about this topic at almost every conference she attended. Matt continued to learn more about special education and law through his trips to Austin, occasionally attending conferences and taking a graduate class in special education. A major portion of the course was on developing measurable IEP goals and objectives.

Both of us read books on negotiation and developed a team approach that we used at IEP meetings. We would discuss our agenda before the IEP meeting, and we began to develop a strategy that would allow us to have some measure of control during the meeting. After an IEP meeting, the two of us would debrief. In the past, we had been so overwhelmed that we had difficulty keeping up with what was being said. We wanted to participate, but we just did not have the information we needed to make a contribution. Our current knowledge and experience allowed us to feel comfortable with expressing our thoughts and, if necessary, challenging statements made by other committee members. We held the IEP members, including ourselves, to a standard that required all of us to support our statements with some form of evidence. This reduced the number of unsolicited opinions that were offered during meetings. These seemed to be more a reflection of a person's attitude than a legitimate and therefore productive contribution to discussions. During the IEP meeting, DeAnn would concentrate on proposing interventions that she had researched or challenging those made by others that did not seem to be appropriate for Ryan. Matt listened closely to what was being said during the meetings; occasionally he would challenge a person who was making statements that were inconsistent or inaccurate. When one of us was speaking, the other would watch the behavior of the other members, to get an idea of how they were receiving the information. Once both of us has taken graduate courses in intelligence and achievement testing, we began to assert ourselves in this area, although our participation did not go over too well with one diagnostician.

During one IEP meeting, Matt noticed that the second-grade teacher voiced several questions about how Ryan learned. We explained as best we could our experience with Ryan as a learner. Matt asked, 'What do you need to be successful with Ryan?' The special education coordinator immediately retorted, 'We are not here to address the teacher's needs, we are here to address Ryan's needs.' Matt turned to the coordinator and said, 'Until we have met Ryan's teacher's needs, she cannot meet my son's needs.' He turned to the teacher and asked the question again. The teacher informed the IEP committee that she was fine. In the future we learned to ask Ryan's teachers this question before the IEP meeting.

As one of us was at the school every day, we became a familiar sight to the teachers and staff, and we began to establish relationships that in some cases later developed into friendships. We came to realize that though we did not always agree, we could always trust the principal to follow through with his word. Our experiences with him and his staff became a turning point in our attitude toward educators. Gradually, we were making the transition from being 'warrior parents' to building productive relationships with the people at our son's school.

At the end of the school year, we had the annual IEP meeting to discuss and agree upon IEP goals and objectives for the following school year. We were introduced to Ryan's teacher for third grade, chosen by the principal. An important point made by the second-grade teacher at this IEP meeting was that Ryan would appear as if he were not paying attention during instruction, but whenever the teacher asked Ryan a question about something she had just said, Ryan could give the correct answer. Throughout the rest of Ryan's school career, most of Ryan's teachers would make this observation. Everyone was pleased with Ryan's progress in the area of social skills development, but the second-grade teacher and the principal expressed their concerns about how he was progressing academically. They recommended that Ryan spend time in content mastery. We recognized the fact that Ryan needed academic assistance, but as we were more interested in his feeling that he was a full member of his class, not just a visitor, as he had been in the previous school district, we rejected the idea of content mastery.

DeAnn had had a conversation with Ryan's occupational therapist before the IEP meeting about his poor handwriting skills. This conversation convinced us that Ryan would benefit from using a computer to complete most writing assignments. We discussed this idea with the other members of the IEP committee and convinced them to agree to an Assistive Technology (AT) evaluation. The principal and teacher were most concerned with Ryan's poor reading skills. We were also concerned about his ability to read because of its impact on all academic areas, so we agreed to have Ryan tested to determine his specific educational needs. The associate psychologist offered to administer the evaluation. He had worked as our parent trainer and in-home trainer during the previous school year. We liked him, but we were apprehensive about his administering the testing because he had told us at the time he began working with Ryan that he had little experience with children who had autism. He also indicated that he would probably recommend placement in a self-contained classroom. Although we had reservations, we agreed to the evaluation, with the stipulation that the Dallas psychologist who had evaluated Ryan before we moved would be brought in as a consultant.

Second grade – summer

DeAnn contacted the special education director about Ryan's reading and was advised to see whether Ryan would qualify for a particular reading program. In June we took Ryan to another elementary school to have him evaluated. After the evaluation, the reading teacher said that she believed that Ryan would benefit from the reading program that had been recommended. An elementary school not far from Ryan's offered the program. Having a bus transport him to and from the other campus, as suggested, would take too much time out of his school day. We talked to the director about making the reading program available to Ryan after his school day. We would provide transportation. The special education director agreed and arranged to have a teacher work with Ryan one-on-one four days a week for forty-five minutes after school.

At the elementary school, the IEP committee recommended that Ryan receive extended school year services (ESYS) for the summer. If the test results indicated that he was a candidate for the proposed reading program, he could also receive reading instruction there. During DeAnn's first conversation with the school principal, he made it clear to her that Ryan would be dismissed from summer school if he did not follow the school rules. Regardless that Ryan was a special education student – he would follow the rules like everyone else.

A week after this conversation, we brought Ryan to the school to have him tested more fully for the reading program. While we were waiting for Ryan to finish, we looked up to see the principal and a gentleman neither of us knew approach the room where we were waiting. Without a word to us, the principal turned and walked back in the direction from which he had come as the stranger walked into the room. He began asking us questions about Ryan's behavior at school and at home. We asked him who he was and who had sent him to speak with us about Ryan. He would only say that it was someone from the school district. His evasiveness put us on our guard. Showing up unannounced did not make us very happy, nor did his description of the aversive techniques he routinely used with children with autism. Ryan had never had a behavior problem at home, nor did we ever receive a report from school about bad behavior.

We contacted the director, and she told us that she knew the person in question. She said that he contracted with the district as a behavioral consultant, but she did not know who had invited him to talk with us about Ryan. We told the special education director that we objected to his methods. We also arranged for a meeting with the director and the principal, as we wanted to discuss the conversation that the principal and DeAnn had had concerning behavior.

During this meeting, the first question we asked the principal was whether or not he had asked for the behavior specialist to talk to us about Ryan's behavior. He said that he did not instruct the specialist to inquire about Ryan's behavior, and he added that the behavior specialist just happened to be on campus. Unsatisfied with his answer, we moved on to the next issue, the conversation he had had with DeAnn where he talked about removing Ryan from his campus if he did not follow the school rules. It was obvious to us that he was not very well informed on special education law, especially the law that governs the removal of a special education student from a school campus. The decision to change the educational placement of a special education student is made by an IEP committee, not any one individual – not even a school principal. The first step in the process is to have an IEP meeting to determine whether there is a link between the behavior and the child's disability. The school is required to make an effort in good faith to provide interventions that address the behavior. This typically takes the form of a written behavior management plan that becomes part of the IEP document. It should come as no surprise that we decided not to have Ryan attend this school. Our experience with this principal made us appreciate Ryan's home school principal even more.

At around the time of our experience with the difficult principal, the two assistive technology professionals completed their assistive technology evaluation. The evaluation report confirmed the need for Ryan to use a computer to complete written assignments. They informed us that Ryan would begin using a computer as soon as one became available. We pointed out that as their assistive technology evaluation showed that Ryan needed a computer to complete written assignments, the school district was obligated to provide access to one. As luck would have it, the principal walked in during our discussion. When we informed him what the assistive technology professionals had just told us, he turned to them and said that if they could not locate a computer, Ryan would use the one from his office. It did not take long for the assistive technology people to locate a computer for Ryan.

During the latter part of the summer we went to Fort Worth for DeAnn to attend a five-day conference on Inclusion for her work. One of the conference participants was the Dallas psychologist who had assessed Ryan the preceeding year – the same one we had insisted the district bring to West Texas as a consultant. We told her our concerns about the associate psychologist assessing Ryan for specific educational needs. The psychologist said that although she did not understand why Ryan was being assessed so soon after she had completed her battery of tests, it would probably be okay.

When we returned home, the associate psychologist, under the supervision of a doctorate-level psychologist, began his evaluation of Ryan. The tests were administered over the course of two or three weeks during late June and July of 1994. We did not understand why it was taking so long to administer an educational evaluation, but we thought that it would be best to allow the professionals to perform the tests they thought would provide the information that was needed. When the following school year began the associate psychologist went to observe Ryan several times in his third-grade classroom. We started to become a little concerned about the length of time the evaluation was taking. It was our hope that the results of the tests would have been available to the IEP committee by the time school started in the fall.

Third grade – fall

Before third grade began, DeAnn took Ryan to the school to meet his new teacher and to visit his new classroom. He would be instructed in one of several portable buildings adjacent to the main school building. Ryan's new teacher commented that she had never worked with a child like Ryan – as his second-grade teacher had said the year before. DeAnn reassured her by saying that she would do fine and gave her some information on Asperger Syndrome and on autism. DeAnn also suggested that she speak with Ryan's second-grade teacher about her experiences with him. The third-grade teacher and the second-grade teacher happened to be good friends, and they had already been discussing Ryan.

The first day of school came and went without incident. The principal had assigned several of the children that were friendly with Ryan in second grade to his new teacher. Ryan reported that having kids that he felt close to in his new classroom felt 'kind of like a cushion.' Ryan's shirts came home intact. We continued to receive parent training and Ryan received in-home training. Ryan also continued receiving sensory integration and speech therapy. Shortly after school started, Ryan began receiving typing instruction and going to a nearby campus after his regular school day for the reading program. Again we settled into the new school year with the supports Ryan needed in place, except for specific instructional interventions that would be developed from the testing by the psychologists.

In early August, DeAnn received a phone call from a parent she remembered meeting in the hall at Ryan's school. The lady introduced herself as the new President for the Parent Teacher Association (PTA) and informed DeAnn that she had been nominated to be an officer of the board for PTA. DeAnn had watched these 'PTA Moms' talking together in the halls after school, but she thought of them as more of a social group. We had been dues-paying members of the PTA since Ryan first began school the previous year. We went to the general meetings and helped at the school parties, but DeAnn had never entertained the idea of becoming a board member. Her first thought was that she was too young to be involved in PTA. She was reminded of her mother and how involved she was with PTA. She had just started graduate school and was concerned about committing herself to more work if she were to accept the nomination. On the other hand, she thought about how this would give her the opportunity to meet other parents. She also realized that PTA moms had some clout on campus because of their high visibility, and this might prove helpful toward the attainment of services for Ryan, so she agreed to the nomination. The president gave DeAnn directions to her home, so that she could attend the next meeting. Ryan accompanied DeAnn and went off to play with the president's son and several other children when they arrived. The group discussed their ongoing projects for about an hour, and then the meeting was adjourned. On the way home from the meeting, Ryan told DeAnn that he had had a fight with the president's son. He said that the argument ended when he punched the boy in the nose. DeAnn dreaded the phone call that she fully expected to receive from the PTA president, but thankfully the call never came. Ryan and the boy ended up becoming best buddies, and they remained friends until the boy and his family moved to another state after the completion of eighth grade.

Around the middle of October, the psychologist from Dallas arrived to observe Ryan at school. Just before lunch, DeAnn met her and the associate psychologist from our school district to discuss the preliminary results of the evaluation. The associate psychologist read his findings, including the Intelligence Quotient (IQ) portion of the evaluation. Ryan's IQ seemed to have mysteriously dropped to the Borderline Mental Retardation range. This was in stark contrast to the IQ score he had been given the previous year, which had resulted in a score that placed him in the middle of the normal range. DeAnn could not believe what she was hearing, so she asked the psychologist from Dallas to explain how Ryan had received the lower IQ score. She stated that the low IQ score that Ryan received on the norm-referenced test simply reflected the fact that he had autism. The psychologist further stated that the score he was given was not an accurate reflection of Ryan's true IQ. Before the meeting adjourned, DeAnn stated that she expected that the IQ score that had just been discussed would not be put on any document bearing Ryan's name. The meeting ended with the associate psychologist agreeing to leave out the scores on his report.

DeAnn's insistence that the IQ scores on Ryan's school documents be omitted was the result of our experience with the Dallas/Fort Worth area school district where Ryan had previously attended school. The first report there described Ryan as slightly mentally retarded. DeAnn had reviewed this evaluation after we had taken a graduate course together on intelligence testing. She discovered that some of the sub-tests had not been administered because Ryan was said to be non-compliant. The shocking part was that the sub-tests that were given were averaged, and this score was recorded as his IQ.

Several weeks later the associate psychologist made an appointment with us to go over the report he had recently finished. We now understood why this report had taken so long to complete. The investment in time must have been considerable. What we had asked for was an educational evaluation in order to address Ryan's specific academic needs. What we received was a 21-page comprehensive evaluation report that included psychological testing. We were rather confused by this, because Ryan had been evaluated the preceding year, and the associate psychologist had a copy of this report. He was also present at the meeting when the recommendation to conduct an educational evaluation was accepted. There had obviously been a misunderstanding as to what the IEP team was asking for when they recommended an evaluation.

After receiving feedback from other professionals trained in administering evaluations, we decided to make an appointment with the supervising psychologist and the associate psychologist to discuss the report. Our initial questions were directed to the associate psychologist concerning his rationale for performing such an extensive evaluation. We explained that the IEP committee was primarily interested in addressing Ryan's inability to read. The evaluation was supposed to identify where things were breaking down educationally. The testing that was done, although extensive, did not produce the information that the IEP team had agreed was necessary to assist Ryan. As the supervising psychologist had not been present at the IEP meeting where testing had been discussed, Matt explained to her that the evaluation that they recently completed was not what the IEP committee had recommended. He told her that the committee had agreed to an educational evaluation that would supply the necessary information to write specific goals and objectives. The Comprehensive Individual Assessment (CIA) that included psychological testing and a speech evaluation just completed was unnecessary because one had been administered the year before. In addition, we disagreed with the results and suggestions listed in the report. Therefore we said that we would not accept putting this document in Ryan's file, which provoked an angry phone call from the special education director who wanted us to accept the report. DeAnn told her that all we had wanted was an educational evaluation. The director paused and said, 'Well, I could have done that with a Brigance.' (The Brigance is a standardized assessment tool and is a criterian-refered test. This means the student's skills are compared to other students in the same grade, i.e. how is Ryan doing academically compared to other third graders?) DeAnn told her that she agreed with her and added that we did not understand why all the testing had been administered in the first place. The director said she would do some checking.

That same day the principal approached us. He seemed to have been waiting for us when we went to pick Ryan up from school. He said he wanted to speak with us, so we accompanied him to his office. As we sat down, he asked us what was going on. We assumed that he must recently have talked with the special education director. We explained to him what had happened with the evaluation. He suggested that we all sit down together to try to resolve the evaluation issue. We agreed to his suggestion, and arrangements were made to meet the following week. Early in the meeting the special education director apologized for the report, but because of the manpower hours expended, she had an interest in somehow making use of it. She showed us a chart containing information taken from the evaluation. She suggested that it be used instead of the report to address Ryan's needs and made part of Ryan's permanent record. We looked at the chart and agreed to have it placed in Ryan's file.

Third grade – spring

During the spring semester of third grade, Ryan began throwing up in the cafeteria. One day, when DeAnn was visiting Ryan at lunchtime, he threw up on a classmate's shoes. When the boy complained to the teacher, she calmly told the child that his shoes could be cleaned off. Another day, when DeAnn and Ryan arrived home after school, he began crying about a cafeteria worker scolding him for getting sick. Ryan asked his mom to call the worker at school and give her one of her 'lectures.' He was accustomed to having his mom confront anyone who wronged her child. DeAnn immediately called the school and spoke with the cafeteria worker, to find out what had happened. This worker had a reputation for being over-zealous when it came to keeping the children's behavior under control. The worker said that Ryan threw up on purpose. DeAnn told the worker that this was uncharacteristic of Ryan, and it was therefore very doubtful that he would try to get sick on purpose. We decided that it would be a good idea to start going up to the cafeteria at lunchtime to see for ourselves what was happening. Every day for about two weeks one or the other of us had lunch with Ryan. Although we had both attempted to convince the principal that our only interest was to resolve the problem of Ryan getting sick, we do not think that he was entirely convinced. We believed that our daily visits to the cafeteria during Ryan's lunchtime made him uncomfortable, and we could not help thinking that his coming by the cafeteria during that time was motivated by our presence.

After a couple of days we decided to have Ryan bring his lunch instead of buying it. This would rule out any possible ill effects from eating the 'government food,' as Ryan called it. He continued to get sick, and we finally realized that it was when Ryan threw his empty lunch sack into the garbage can that he felt ill and sometimes vomited. When the students finished their lunch, they would enter a small enclosure to discard what remained on their food trays into a row of garbage cans. When we entered the enclosure, we found the odor to be overwhelming. The solution was that Ryan would throw his lunch bag away when he went back to his classroom. Ryan followed our suggestion, and there were no further problems with vomiting in the school cafeteria.

Together, we began preparing for the next annual IEP meeting to decide what supports and services would be provided to Ryan in fourth grade. We were in the habit of sitting down with the previous year's IEPs, reviewing goals and objectives and assessing Ryan's progress toward meeting these. We would do our research and discuss what we would request for the following school year. One day we went to the school to look at Ryan's file to check to see that our facts were correct before presenting them to the IEP committee. It was necessary to ask the diagnostician to see Ryan's file. While we were in her office, she nicely told us that she would prefer that parents allow educators to do their job without the benefit of parent input. We knew that this thinly veiled comment was directed at us. This would not be the only comment she would make to us, expressing her displeasure with our 'interfering' in what she believed to be her business. We chose not to respond to her comments because we knew that they conveyed an attitude that we were not going to change. We also knew that we were entitled by law to be party to any and all educational decisions made concerning our son. She was obviously having difficulty accepting this fact, and we were aware that she was not alone in her thinking. On the other hand, we believe that most of the educators we have experienced accepted us as legitimate members of the IEP team.

The annual IEP meeting was held in early May. After the issues concerning Ryan's education had been discussed, we explained to the IEP committee that we felt that we no longer needed the weekly parent training that had been provided through the school district. We believed that attending the Statewide Annual Autism Conference, put on by the Texas Education Agency (TEA), would be of greater benefit to us. DeAnn explained that we had applied for a stipend to pay for the conference registration and the hotel. The only cost to the school district would be to reimburse us for traveling to Austin. Our plan was to drive our own vehicle, so the cost to the district would be minimal compared to the cost of continuing to provide parent training on a weekly basis. The sum of money we were requesting was equivalent to the cost for the district to provide one hour of parent training for two weeks. After some initial resistance to the idea, we convinced the committee to accept our proposal. During this meeting we also discussed the results of a water therapy evaluation that had taken place in January. The therapist determined that Ryan was too advanced for the services typically offered through the district's program. She did, on the other hand, recommend that he receive swimming lessons to work on occupational therapy issues, including the enhancement of gross motor skills. When Matt proposed that Ryan receive swimming lessons through the YWCA, at the district's expense, the special education coordinator objected. She stated: 'I would prefer to see the taxpayers' money better spent.' We reminded her of what she already knew, or should know: it was entirely inappropriate and violated TEA policy to bring up the issue of money while discussing services and supports to address a student's individual needs.

We decided to write a letter to the special education director by certified mail, informing her of the comment made by the special education coordinator about 'spending taxpayers' money.' The letter communicated the fact that we did not appreciate her interjecting this personal comment during our son's IEP meeting. First of all, swimming instruction was recommended by the water therapist to address occupational therapy issues. As the recommendation came from a specialist employed by the school, there should not have been an objection to the school paying for the service. The school district received federal money to pay for special education services. The cost to the district for the service would be very low when compared to the amount of money paid to the occupational therapists or water therapists for providing direct services. The YWCA was going to require a membership in the amount of thirty dollars for the entire school year. The instruction would be provided at a rate of only four dollars per hour once a week. We were planning to provide transportation to and from the YWCA. To this day we do not think that our request for swimming lessons was excessive, especially given the fact that during the time he was receiving instruction, we observed Ryan making progress. For a child like Ryan it was not merely 'swimming lessons' – it was a valuable and much-needed related service intended to enhance his coordination. His problems were obvious, and he demonstrated a need for this kind of service whenever he walked or ran. When walking, he would hold his arms stiffly to his sides; when he ran, his hands were raised stiffly to the height of his chest.

The director responded with her own certified letter. In the letter she did not address swimming. Instead, she informed us that she had conducted a survey of 60 school districts, and none of the districts surveyed sent parents to conferences outside their region. This was a clear message that she thought we were being unreasonable when we requested travel expenses to the conference. Our letter responded to the director's letter by reminding her that the IEP committee had agreed to pay our travel expenses to the conference. The last thing we wrote – and probably should have left off – was that if she wanted to influence the outcome of one of our son's IEP meetings, she needed to attend.

We understood that the director was operating her department with a limited budget, and she might think that she was setting a precedent for services for other families. She had every reason to know that there was little collective knowledge in the area about what interventions were needed and how to provide them. We were entering uncharted territory, as Asperger Syndrome was a new diagnosis in *The Diagnostic and Statistical Manual Fourth Edition* (DSM-IV, 1994). Though Ryan did not have an official diagnosis of Asperger Syndrome, we knew that this explained Ryan's behavior. Many students with Asperger Syndrome had previously been diagnosed with ADHD (attention defecit hyperactivity disorder), PDD-NOS, or other related disorders. The director began to attend Ryan's IEP meetings more often, and when she did come, although we did not always agree with her, she proved to be an asset. Having taken a genuine interest in Ryan, she provided valuable information and helpful suggestions that proved to be beneficial to him.

Matt picked Ryan up from summer school every day. He would sit in the reception area in front of the principal's office and read while he waited. The teacher walked Ryan up to the office when it was time for him to leave. The principal was the one who had suggested that Matt wait there for Ryan. One day, as Matt sat waiting for Ryan, the phone rang in the principal's office. The principal answered the phone and began talking. Where Matt was sitting, he could clearly hear the principal when he spoke with the person on the phone. It became clear who it was that he was talking to and who he was talking about. It was the special education director who was conversing with the principal, and judging by his responses, it seemed clear that she was complaining about us. Matt was in a quandary; if he got up and left, the principal would see him. If he stayed, it would appear as if he was eavesdropping. He decided to remain seated, because the principal was fully aware that Matt waited in the reception area for Ryan each day and would be able to hear his telephone conversation. The principal calmly told the director that he liked us and he supported us completely. After the phone call, the principal came out of his office and smiled at Matt. He proved to be a straight shooter, and he turned out to be one of our greatest allies.

We did attend the state autism conference with the district reimbursing us for the mileage, as the IEP committee had agreed. The conference turned out to be highly informative and extremely beneficial to both of us. Never again did we agree to parent training in our home or through the district. We were fortunate to continue to find methods of attending future conferences. It is still our opinion that the state conference was not only more cost-effective, but also appropriate for our parent training.

What we learned

During these years, the two of us learned that we could trust educators. However, we also began to realize that the education system was a business. One of the most important lessons we learned was the importance of establishing relationships with the people who worked with our son. In the beginning, our relationship with the elementary school staff was one filled with skepticism and mistrust. From our experience with the school staff in the Dallas/Fort Worth area, we had learned to proceed with decisions in the IEP committee with a great deal of caution. We had been deceived in the past, and we were not about to be deceived again.

As we began experiencing the West Texas elementary school staff, we discovered that we had stumbled across a group of individuals who truly wanted Ryan to succeed. Though we were sometimes at odds (e.g., we wanted social skills development, the campus staff wanted academics), we did manage to find a middle ground, balancing, as best we could, Ryan's social and academic needs. We continued to be assertive and to stand up for Ryan's rights. However, we also began to let down our defenses, so that we could work with the school staff in a more relaxed manner. As the two of us began to relax, we noticed that the principal and the teachers became more at ease with us. Eventually, we formed a close relationship with the staff. We were finally able to transcend our bad experiences from the previous school and move forward.

This was also a time of great creativeness for working with Ryan. The teachers and the therapists all developed methods of working with him to increase his social skills. Activities such as the Fun Club helped Ryan to form friendships while developing communication skills. The teachers grouped Ryan with children who were accepting of him, which also helped him to develop friendships while acquiring social skills. Ryan, his teachers, and his therapists also developed close relationships.

During the time that Matt was part of an Inclusion pilot program, he would sometimes go to the teachers' lounge to have coffee and read educator periodicals. He learned that historically general education teachers did not receive the support they needed to be successful in teaching special needs children. As a result of this, they had little expectation of receiving the help – such as in-service training on specific disabilities – that they needed. Matt's experience, in addition to the special education coordinator expressing that the IEP committee was responsible for Ryan's needs, not the teacher's needs, provided us with insight into the realities of the education system. When we recognized that education was a business, we came to the realization that there were gatekeepers who would attempt to limit the district's commitment to provide services. In an effort to attain Ryan's educational needs and also the classroom teacher's needs, we began meeting with Ryan's teachers before the IEP meeting. At these pre-IEP meetings we discussed the teacher's concerns and drafted IEP goals and objectives. This was helpful for several reasons: (1) the teacher and we were on the same page by the time we had the official meeting, (2) we could push for the supports the teacher needed, and (3) the teacher and we could present a united front. We continued this practice throughout the elementary and junior high years. We also began talking to the therapists beforehand.

Even though we developed a high level of trust with the campus staff, inevitably from time to time we encountered difficult people. We were told by a diagnostician in no uncertain terms that we should go home and stay out of the school's business. She was very clear that she did not consider us equal participants in the process – quite to the contrary, we interfered with her doing her job. There were others who were not as blatant but condescending to us as parents. Their actions and their words told us explicitly that we were not considered equal participants. Because Asperger Syndrome was relatively unknown when we moved to West Texas, we continued to encounter uninformed professionals. Many would be up front and tell us that they were not knowledgeable about Asperger Syndrome, but others were not so willing to share the limitations of their knowledge, and this led to much conflict between the professionals and us.

On the other hand, because of these difficult people, we were both put in a position to continue to learn about Asperger Syndrome, appropriate interventions, education law, and negotiation. Often we walked a fine line between being assertive while not alienating the people who were allies. We took graduate-level classes in writing IEPs and evaluation. Soon we were as well informed (and in some cases more informed) as the educators in the IEP meetings. By developing these skills, we were ensuring that Ryan was receiving the appropriate education that he deserved. The difficult people also gave us an incentive to continue to research Asperger Syndrome, and even though the available information was limited, through our research and our intuition we developed creative and effective ways of working with Ryan.

This was a time of great insight and personal growth for us both. We developed negotiation skills that have helped in all aspects of our lives. We increased our knowledge of the education system and how to get the school system to provide appropriate services and supports for our son. As our skills grew, so did our self-confidence. We learned to rely on our knowledge and our instincts. We discovered a group of people at the elementary school who were dedicated to working with children. The principal and his staff were passionate about working with Ryan. The elementary school staff and the two of us managed to bridge the chasm between family and school. As a result, they helped us heal from our negative experiences with the previous school district.

What you can do

- It takes many meetings to get the child the services he/she needs. Take small steps. Focus on the one or two most important services at the meeting. When you have achieved those, then go on to the next most important two or three. Don't try to solve all the issues in one meeting.

- When writing goals and objectives, determine your goals for the student. For example, is the student in math class for math or for developing social skills? Is the student writing an assignment for written expression or for penmanship? Write your goals accordingly.

- Become familiar with various therapies (e.g., occupational therapy, sensory integration, assistive technology).

- Identify sensory issues: either remove the negative sensory problem or identify interventions for coping with it.

- Do not assume that a student with sensory problems is not paying attention. These students can have a difficult time with attending behavior – e.g., sitting up at desk, looking at teacher. Check periodically to see whether the student is listening.

- Be creative with speech therapy. Typical children should be involved in the therapy to help develop language pragmatics.

- Learn the laws that govern special education.

- Read books on negotiation skills, and develop those skills.

- Practice your negotiation and listening skills.

- Be familiar with various teaching methodologies.

- Bring your research to the meetings. Support your requests with facts.

- Learn the laws that govern parent participation in your child's education.

- Attend workshops on your rights as parents in the educational system.

- Become familiar with the rules regarding what information on your child is confidential, and how the records are to be kept.
- Build relationships with the people who work with your child.
- Work together as a team in the meetings.
- Look through the child's school folder on a regular basis.
- Be visible on the child's campus (e.g., Parent Teacher Association, volunteer work).
- Check regularly with the teacher and principal.
- Learn the agencies that have advocates and to identify those who can help you to understand the education process.
- Meet with teachers and therapists before the IEP meeting to draft goals and objectives.
- Find medical professionals who are willing to learn about your child's special needs and who are accepting of the child's issues.

Tips for parents and professionals for successful IEP meetings

- Show a positive body language:
  - stand or sit straight;
  - sit in a relaxed, businesslike manner;
  - look people in the eye when speaking;
  - keep eye contact while conversing with the others;
  - *ALWAYS* be courteous, pleasant, and respectful.
- Get copies of all of the child's records.

- Research your specific concerns (e.g., why your request is educationally necessary for the child.)

- Come organized.

- Bring your research and information with you.

- Have information you need where you can easily locate it.

- Flag and highlight the information you need for easy access.

- Make sure your requests are reasonable; research your requests thoroughly.

- If the school refuses or disagrees with you, have them write down why they disagree or refuse.

- Listen with the intention of learning.

- Submit your requests in writing.

- Remember: the school district is only responsible for providing the services and modifications that are written in the school paperwork.

- Ask as many questions as necessary. Try to frame your questions so that they are not confrontational.

- Take notes during the meeting. When you hear something you want more information about, write it down. This will free you up to listen, as opposed to trying to remember what was said. You can come back to your question later.

- Come with an agenda of items you want to discuss. This includes your questions.

- When you ask a question, be sure to write down the answer you are given. Often a question that has been asked will end up not being answered because another issue is brought up. You can then see that you have not written down the answer, and you will know to repeat the question until it is answered.

Chapter Four

Grades Four through Six

Fourth grade

Shortly before the fourth-grade school year began, we were notified that the teacher chosen by the principal to instruct Ryan had moved from the area because her husband had been transferred. The teacher Ryan had had for math in summer school was chosen to take her place. This turned out very well, because she had already worked with Ryan and she proved to be a very competent teacher. As in previous years, DeAnn took Ryan to his new classroom to show him where he would be sitting. During the visit, the teacher mentioned that before she had taught Ryan for a brief time during the summer, she had not worked with a child like him. DeAnn assured her that everything would be fine, as she had done with Ryan's second- and third-grade teachers, and also supplied her with information on Asperger Syndrome and autism and extended our offer of support. As luck would have it, the fourth-grade teacher and Ryan's two previous teachers were good friends. They had already exchanged information about their experiences with Ryan and with us.

The fourth grade was much more difficult for Ryan. The academic demands of reading and math seemed much greater than in previous years. The social demands were also much greater. We knew that he was feeling the pressure when he began to detach himself from what was going on in the classroom. His teacher informed us of a new behavior that Ryan started to exhibit in the classroom. He began giggling for no apparent reason. We immediately realized he was 'self-stimming' (self-stimulating) or stimming. What she did not know is that Ryan, by his report, had been stimming at school since the second grade back in the Dallas/Fort Worth area. He had learned to hide the fact that he was doing it, but teachers would sometimes catch him.

Ryan began to develop a liking for the slapstick humor of the Three Stooges. In a relatively short period he accumulated an extensive collection of Stooges movies. He would watch them over and over again and would mimic some of the behaviors he saw on film. At first we were happy that he enjoyed watching them so much. He would laugh so hard that his sides would ache. He acted out some of the behaviors he had seen in the movies in front of his friends. Initially the children would laugh at his performances, but they soon tired of them. They began showing their impatience nonverbally, but Ryan was not picking up the signs. Some of the children would occasionally voice their intolerance. When this occurred, Ryan would make adjustments. We began to coach him on interpreting the children's body language to help him recognize the signs that would inform him that his humor was not appreciated.

Our efforts to instruct Ryan on reading body language are a continuing task. He has made measurable progress over the years, but at the time we had to rely on our powers of persuasion. We appealed to his intellect and his trust in our judgment to get him to stop his slapstick behavior. We managed to convince him that although it was funny in the beginning, it was now annoying to the people around him. First we had to get him into the habit of watching other people's behavior, because he was not accustomed to doing this. Then we started talking with him about what he thought others were thinking and feeling. As Ryan's slapstick humor decreased, a new form of humor emerged to take its place. He started telling jokes. What he did not understand at the beginning is that you can usually only tell the same joke to someone once. Ryan had a habit of telling the same joke several times to the same audience. It took him a while to understand and accept that people might be put off by this practice. He would then need only occasional reminders about his having already told a joke to the same audience. The next step in his evolution as a joke teller was to come up with variations on the jokes he was telling. Although he himself had trouble containing his laughter when telling the variations, they just were not funny. With each variation it was necessary to explain to him why the new joke did not get the response of the original. Our continuing discussions with him about what makes a joke humorous helped him to develop his understanding. He now has a repertoire of jokes to draw upon. He has a tendency, with the jokes he knows well, to rattle them off in quick succession without giving his audience time to process the information. Although he continues to need some assistance with telling jokes, he has made a great deal of progress.

It was no doubt as a result of his exposure to typical boyish behavior that Ryan learned that he could get a laugh out of his classmates when he made noises with his body. We later learned that the behavior was typical of boys Ryan's age. One of the primary reasons for our insistence that Ryan experience a general education classroom was to learn from typical children. This was one of those behaviors that we would have preferred he did not learn. Ryan would join in with other boys who were making body noises during class time. One day when the teacher had enough of their behavior, she sent them to the principal's office. He had a talk with them about making the noises, then sent them back to class.

Ryan casually conveyed the event to DeAnn the same day. He told her that he and the other boys had not gotten in to trouble. They had been sent to the office to talk with the principal to *avoid* getting into trouble. This was the only time Ryan had ever been sent to the principal's office because of a behavioral problem. The teacher told us later that the principal gave the boys a warning to discourage future incidents. Since Ryan had a tendency to adhere to rules strictly, he did not repeat this behavior at school. Instead, he started doing it at home. It was necessary to make it a rule to get him to stop.

The assistive technologist began working with Ryan when third grade began. It was a tough beginning. Ryan would get very frustrated with this person and was not very cooperative. When he was questioned recently about this experience, Ryan said, 'I started getting rough with him because he made me work.' One day Ryan asked the technologist what he would do if Ryan threw up on him. According to the teacher who overheard the comment, the assistive technologist did not know how to respond and was obviously uncomfortable with the thought. Eventually, they managed to work things out, and Ryan started taking an interest in typing later that fall. He received a certification the following spring for being the best typist in the school. He was beginning to use the computer for his schoolwork. We were told that the teacher also began teaching Ryan how to use the calculator. The technology helped Ryan to gain new skills in class. His reading and math both continued to improve.

Several of the children in the class had been with Ryan since second grade. They were protective of him and showed a lot of patience with his unusual behavior. When they were tired of him talking about the same subject over and over again, which is a type of perseverating that is typical for individuals with Asperger Syndrome, they had learned just to ignore it. On one occasion when Matt was driving the Fun Club children home, Ryan began talking about something that he had obviously been talking about earlier. One of the children told Ryan, using a matter-of-fact tone, that she was tired of hearing him talk about the subject. After dropping off the last child, Matt asked Ryan how he felt about what she had said. Ryan's response indicated that he was neither hurt nor offended by the comment. We found out that some of the other children were beginning to speak out when Ryan talked on and on about one of his favorite topics. As a result, he began to perseverate on his favorite topics less at school. To encourage friendships, we sometimes went to visit an acquaintance who had an old paint pony named MoJo. Ryan's new in-home trainer knew her and made the arrangements. Children outside the Fun Club heard about the trips to visit the horse. This worked quite well, because more children began interacting with Ryan, and this gave him more opportunities to practice his social skills.

Ryan's speech therapist had taken a special interest in Ryan. She asked if she could spend time with him after school hours. We needed someone to watch Ryan for us one night a week while we were both in class. We knew her and trusted her, so we were excited about her offer. Because we were so far from our own family, she became Ryan's surrogate grandmother. She began taking Ryan out into the community, working with him on his social skills in the process.

One day, while DeAnn was in the diagnostician's office, she noticed that two boys were eating lunch at her table. She also saw that her file cabinet, where all the special education records were stored, was unlocked. As DeAnn left the office, she asked why the boys were there, and she was told that they were being punished. When she asked whether they were being closely supervised, she was told that they were not. DeAnn immediately checked with the diagnostician about the unlocked file cabinet, and she was informed that the cabinet was never locked. When DeAnn told her that other students were in her office as a form of punishment, she answered that she was not concerned. DeAnn then talked with the principal. He said that the cabinet would be kept locked.

Two weeks later, when she was in the diagnostician's office again, DeAnn noticed that the cabinet was not locked. She returned home, called the Texas Education Agency (TEA), and asked about the standard for locking file cabinets with special education student records. The TEA attorney asked her to describe the setting of the file cabinet. When DeAnn finished, he told her that we had grounds for a complaint and asked whether she would like to file one. DeAnn told him that she would give the information to the principal and that she was sure that he would take care of the problem. She then contacted the principal and repeated what the TEA attorney had told her. There was silence on the other end of the phone for a few moments. Then the principal said, 'You know, DeAnn, a few people would be intimidated about what you just did.' DeAnn assured him that she just wanted to make sure she was correct about the file cabinet, so she had called to check her facts. The principal said that the cabinet would be kept locked.

During the spring of fourth grade, DeAnn was taking a Foundations in Reading class; the course dealt with different types of reading problems and interventions. Based on the current research on reading, it seemed that the reading methodology that Ryan had been using was one of the slowest ways of teaching students how to read. DeAnn began to investigate the reading program that Ryan had been attending for two years. These two years had involved us taking Ryan to another campus after school four days a week for 45 minutes each session. We had also taken him to the reading program four days a week each summer.

Disturbed about the new information regarding reading interventions, DeAnn asked to see the reading program manual. She found that the program had been developed for students of English as a second language and for children with mental retardation. When we had agreed to enroll Ryan in the program, we had been told that he would only need it for one year. One year then turned into two. This time, when DeAnn asked two of the reading teachers at what point Ryan would be finished, she was told he had two more years. DeAnn asked how many students had ever completed the program. The two reading teachers told DeAnn that they had never known any student to finish completely – they just went into Junior High and stopped using the program.

DeAnn approached her professor, who had many years of experience as a reading teacher and called herself a reading specialist, and asked if she would assess Ryan's reading. The professor assessed Ryan and discovered the problem. Ryan had a 'top-down' processing problem, which meant that he was not reading every word; he was skipping words and making up what he was reading as he went along. The solution was to have Ryan read directions and information with specific details that he could not skip. For example, DeAnn would have Ryan follow recipes to cook foods he liked. We pulled Ryan out of the reading program and began working with him ourselves. His reading improved substantially. We had thought that Ryan had received a reading evaluation when he was tested two years earlier. What we learned is that the teacher had given him an evaluation to see whether he was a candidate for the program. Instead of evaluating Ryan to see where his reading skills broke down and then providing the appropriate reading intervention, the school offered a program that was already in place but did not address his individual needs. As is turned out, the reading program Ryan had been involved in at school did not provide a productive intervention for his particular reading problem. This was another hard lesson for us. Because we lacked the information we needed at the time of the 'evaluation,' Ryan did not make the progress in reading we believe he would have made with another, more suitable program.

At the end of fourth grade, the principal decided that he would retire. We were heartbroken. Before he left, he made arrangements to have Ryan attend the class of the teacher he had chosen. He warned DeAnn that she was a very strict teacher, but an excellent one. She was not one to hug a lot, and she had a personality quite different from the rest of the teachers. He then jokingly said that maybe the fact that she was from Nebraska would explain her being different. DeAnn laughed and said, 'Then we will get along just fine, because I'm from Nebraska.' This teacher not only turned out to be a very good teacher, but she also became a good friend of ours.

As mandated by federal law, a special education student must be given an evaluation every three years to establish eligibility. We both knew that Ryan's three-year evaluation was coming soon. As a result of our experience with the last evaluation, we decided to get one on our own. DeAnn approached Ryan's pediatrician and asked for a recommendation to get a neuropsychological evaluation. A friend of DeAnn's who had met Ryan had come across an article about Nonverbal Learning Disabilities (NLD) that made it sound very similar to Asperger Syndrome. It was published by the Yale Child Study Center and also included a questionnaire parents could complete. They were conducting a study on NLD, and if your child qualified, you could get an evaluation from Yale. DeAnn had sent in the information, but in the meantime we made the appointment for a neuropsychological assessment and took Ryan in for his evaluation.

A practicum student working on his doctorate in psychology administered the tests, under the supervision of his professor. DeAnn brought articles on Asperger Syndrome for the student to read. We knew that when he read them, they would help to convince him that Ryan had Asperger Syndrome. Because of our last evaluation scare and as DeAnn had taken an evaluation course, she sat in on all the tests and watched to make sure that they were administered correctly. The intern seemed to accept her presence. DeAnn explained that the intern was to give Ryan regular breaks, and to tell Ryan exactly how much he was expected to complete. She also informed the intern that we did not want Intelligence Quotient (IQ) scores; we wanted the report in a descriptive format. After many days of evaluation and writing the report, the intern sat down with us with his findings. Once again, we expected Ryan to be diagnosed with Asperger Syndrome. Once again, we were disappointed. He diagnosed high-functioning autism because he felt that Ryan's speech had been delayed when he was a child. We both felt that he had misunderstood the intent of the DSM-IV. No amount of discussion would convince him to reconsider. The recommendations were very good, so we took the report to the school and informed them that Ryan's three-year evaluation had been completed.

Fifth grade

The principal at Ryan's school retired the summer before fifth grade began. From the beginning we had liked this man, and we sorely missed his presence – as did probably all of the teaching staff. He was just that kind of guy. An assistant principal from another elementary school in the district replaced him. Matt had had a couple of short conversations with her when he was part of an Inclusion project at the school where she had worked. Unaware that he was a parent of a child with special needs, she had shared with him her opinion that students with special needs should be in special classes. We also found out from both parents and teachers that she had a reputation of orchestrating the removal of special needs children from general education classrooms. Needless to say, we were not happy to learn that she would be our next principal. We disagreed about whether to transfer Ryan to another campus or to keep him where he was. Matt was counting on the positive relationships we had developed to carry us through the two remaining years of primary school.

We were fortunate that the fifth-grade teacher was good friends with the second-, third-, and fourth-grade teachers. The fifth-grade teacher told us that she had never worked with a child like Ryan, and once again we reassured her that everything would be fine. Over a period of time Ryan developed a very close friendship with this teacher; he responded very well to her strict approach to teaching and her highly structured classroom.

On the first day of school the new principal stopped DeAnn as she was leaving the building with Ryan and said that Ryan typing his work on the computer would bother the other students. Ryan had a computer program that spoke the words as he typed them, and she thought that he and his computer should be moved to the content mastery room. DeAnn informed her that the IEP committee had decided that Ryan would use his computer in the classroom, but the principal responded that the computer would be moved the following day. DeAnn went home and immediately called the special education director and relayed her conversation with the principal. DeAnn told the director that at the most recent IEP meeting the assistive technologist had recommended that the computer be used in the classroom and we supported her staff; she finished by saying that we hoped that the matter would be handled rather than having it turn into a problem. The director was aware of the legal ramifications of the principal carrying out her plan to remove the computer and knew what DeAnn meant about it turning into a problem. We would use all means at our disposal to see that the principal's action would not stand, along with notifying the TEA. The following morning DeAnn took Ryan to school as usual. The principal met DeAnn and Ryan at the door and sweetly informed DeAnn that the computer would remain in the classroom. DeAnn thanked her.

Ryan continued to giggle quietly during class, for no apparent reason. When his teacher noticed this behavior, she would get his attention, and he would get back on task. Although she was successful in redirecting him, the giggling continued. When she brought the problem to our attention, we questioned him about it. He said, 'I am running Three Stooges tapes through my head.' Because of the impact it was having on his education, we wanted to know how often he was self-stimming. We convinced the IEP committee to allow the use of a video camera to capture the frequency rate of the behavior. The camera was turned on for one hour each day for a period of one week. We viewed the tape with the teacher and were amazed at how often Ryan was stimming.

DeAnn had to come up with a research project for the Applied Behavior Analysis class she was taking. She had just finished a semester of learning how to teach the Lovaas method – an intensive behavioral treatment method for young children on the autism spectrum. After her experience with the Lovaas method, she decided to use a self-monitoring and self-graphing technique, with Ryan as her subject. DeAnn had noticed during her observations of him in the classroom that he would put his head down on his desk and quietly giggle. DeAnn developed a program where he began to keep track of when he was putting his head on his desk. There was a dramatic reduction in the stimming behavior, which we attribute to the self-graphing method Ryan employed. Allowing Ryan to self-stim at home may also have helped to reduce the frequency. The behavior, by Ryan's report, peaked in fifth grade, but it continued at school until some time during the seventh grade. Ryan informed us that he would sometimes stim in seventh grade because he was nervous around the teaching assistant.

Early in the fall, a friend of DeAnn's, who worked at the education service center, called and told us that she and another service center employee had just been given a tour of Ryan's school by the principal. DeAnn's friend had only met Ryan once before, but she recognized him. She went on to tell DeAnn that the principal had noticed her staring at Ryan and stated, 'That's Ryan, our little autistic boy.' The two service center employees were speechless. Not only had this principal made the mistake of announcing Ryan's name and his disorder (which violated the law) – she had done so in the presence of our son. The friend asked us not to let anyone know what she had just told us, and after discussing the situation, we decided to let the matter drop. To have pursued it would have caused DeAnn's friend problems, and it would not help Ryan. But the attitude the principal conveyed was not lost on us, and we were not at all happy about it.

One day in the fall Matt received a phone call from Ryan's content mastery teacher about something Ryan was reported to have done. The IEP committee had agreed that if there was a problem having to do with Ryan's behavior, we would be notified before any disciplinary action was taken. She informed Matt that Ryan had broken another student's ruler, and she wanted to know what they should do. Matt asked to speak with Ryan, so she put him on the phone. He was crying. Matt told Ryan that he would take care of the matter, and everything would be ok. This seemed to calm Ryan down. When Ryan was ready, he explained that he and a friend had been looking at another student's ruler. Then his friend began bending the ruler, until it was broken. Afterwards she told everyone that Ryan had broken the ruler. Ryan then told Matt, 'You know I would not have broken it on purpose because it was blue.' With this information and Ryan's history, Matt knew that

Ryan was telling the truth. The color blue was one of the topics Ryan perseverated on. His reverence for the color would not allow him to intentionally harm any object that was blue. Matt told Ryan that he was not in trouble and to hand the phone back to his teacher. Matt informed her that he believed that Ryan had not broken the ruler, and he briefly explained why. He also inquired about witnesses to the act. He was told that the teacher had been absent from the room at the time of the incident, and the only person who said she saw Ryan break the ruler was his accuser. This bright young lady with a pleasing personality had befriended Ryan, so it was difficult to imagine her saying that Ryan had broken the ruler if it was not true. Given that there was only the one witness and the fact that the ruler was blue, Matt told the content mastery teacher that there was insufficient evidence to punish Ryan. She agreed to take no action against Ryan.

When Matt told DeAnn the story, she went to the school to talk to his teacher. DeAnn learned that the problem had occurred in the general education classroom, so she talked to that teacher. DeAnn asked to see the ruler. She was shown a cheap blue plastic ruler that was broken in half. It could be purchased at a variety of stores for about fifty cents. The teacher told DeAnn that the ruler had been given to its owner by his great-grandfather. The significance of the ruler to the boy was measured by the fact that it was the last thing given to him by his great-grandfather, who had recently passed away. The ruler had a clean break and could be mended, so DeAnn asked the boy if it would be okay for Ryan's dad to repair it, and he answered, 'yes.' DeAnn told him that she would buy him another ruler, just like the one that was broken, for school and she suggested that he keep his great-grandfather's ruler at home. The boy said that he would. He then proceeded to tell DeAnn that he saw the ruler being broken by the girl who had accused Ryan. By

Ryan's report, the children in his class and the teachers believed that he had broken the ruler, even though he denied it.

We knew the girl and her family well. She was one of the children in the Fun Club with Ryan, and her mother had been active in the PTA. We expected to receive a phone call from the mother that evening, because it was likely that the little girl would talk to her mom about the incident with the ruler, and at about 9:00 p.m. the mother called and asked what had happened. DeAnn explained what we knew at the time. The mother said that her daughter was crying when she got home. She was upset about falsely accusing Ryan, when she was the one who had broken the ruler. The girl explained to her mother that she had only one slip left. The school used a slip system for discipline. The first slip that would be pulled was green, the second yellow, and the last red. When the red slip was pulled, there was a consequence to the behavior. The girl knew that when her last slip was pulled, she would be punished at school and receive a spanking at home. Ryan did not use the slip system because he perseverated all day on getting one pulled, and this made it very difficult for him to concentrate on his schoolwork. The girl told her mom that breaking the ruler was an accident. She had blamed Ryan because she thought he would not get into trouble because he did not pull slips.

The following day we all met with the teacher at school. We went to a private room, where the teary-eyed young lady apologized to Ryan. Ryan accepted her apology and then said that 'This is something you do to your enemies, not your friends.' This statement caused her to start crying. If it had been someone other than Ryan who made the rather callous statement, one might think that there was malicious intent. Since it was Ryan, we believe that the statement can be attributed primarily to his Asperger Syndrome. He would not deliberately hurt her feelings, and apparently he did not realize how upset she was. Ryan told us that he was confused by what she had done. He thought she had made an error, and he wished to correct her by making the point. He said that he wanted her to know to do it to someone she did not like in the future. Ryan said that he continues to think of her as a friend.

The teachers must have felt that they were between the proverbial 'rock and a hard place.' We asked Ryan why he thought the teacher would have believed the girl instead of him. He said, 'It was probably because she did not act as nervous as me.' He said that as the day progressed, he became more and more nervous and actually began to entertain the thought that he had broken the ruler. In his words, 'Sureness faded away as the day wore on.' He was asked by the content mastery teacher to look at her and tell her that he did not break the ruler, but he could not. Ryan said, 'I couldn't because of self-doubt...I was nervous.' A couple of his classmates had told him that he needed to tell the truth. He also made the statement that 'one person's mind can easily be swayed by a group.' He obviously had a great deal of trouble processing the events that occurred.

Later in the spring, DeAnn received a phone call from a doctoral student at the local university. The student immediately started asking questions about Ryan. The questions were extremely personal, coming from someone we had never met or heard of. DeAnn would not answer her questions. When the doctoral student was asked who had made arrangements for her to observe Ryan in school she would only say that it was someone from special education. DeAnn left work and went to the school; she talked with Ryan's general education teacher and the content mastery teacher. They said that they had cautioned the doctoral student when she had arrived to obverve Ryan that she needed to call us first before she would be allowed in the classroom. The teachers did not allow the doctoral student to conduct her observation. They knew we would be unhappy to learn that someone had observed Ryan without our prior knowledge. DeAnn thanked them for contacting us beforehand.

Ryan was not observed without our permission again. We later learned from an outside source that the two teachers had been reprimanded for not letting the doctoral student observe Ryan and for telling us about it. Ryan now has instructions to tell us if anyone appears to be observing him at school.

We began to notice during fifth grade that Ryan was falling further and further behind socially. The number of children in his class who seemed to accept Ryan's odd behavior began to dwindle. One day Ryan came home from school in tears. It was obvious that his feelings had been hurt. DeAnn questioned Ryan about what had happened and who was involved, and she was shocked to hear that a boy Ryan considered to be his best friend and another boy whom he had known for two years had told him to shut up and go away. DeAnn talked to the mothers of the two boys, and the situation was never repeated. However, it was a clear signal to us that even Ryan's closest friends were starting to drift away from him. This incident marked the beginning of a trend toward isolation. The boys can hardly be blamed for not wanting to share their time with Ryan. They were operating on a different wavelength and no longer had much in common with him. As time went on, the social demands of being a teenager became further and further beyond Ryan's abilities. We watched, helplessly – as his circle of friends became smaller and smaller.

Around the end of fifth grade we began to think about the transition to junior high. At the annual IEP meeting we discussed with the other committee members the recommendation that Ryan have a teaching assistant (e.g., paraprofessional) to work with him in the classroom. The recommendation came from the neuropsychological evaluation administered during the summer before fifth grade. We had not pushed this intervention because the fifth-grade teacher had strongly objected to having a teaching assistant in her classroom. Having the teaching assistant begin working with Ryan in sixth grade would allow sufficient time for this person to learn about Ryan's needs and how he operated. We thought that this would be an effective way to ease the transition to junior high. The IEP committee agreed to the recommendation for a teaching assistant, and a few days after the meeting the principal introduced us to the person she had chosen for the job.

Sixth grade

Sixth grade began, as had the preceding grades, with the teacher stating that he had never worked with a child like Ryan. This time DeAnn arranged for him to sit down with all of Ryan's previous teachers to discuss Ryan and their experiences with him. The new teacher was given assurances by his colleagues that Ryan would not pose any challenges he could not overcome, and the teachers also informed him that he would receive the support of the Foleys.

School was in session for only two weeks before we had a disagreement with the new teaching assistant. When he was introduced to us, we were told, among other things, that he had been a classroom teacher. It seemed curious for him now to be employed as a teaching assistant, but we did not think too much about it at the time. We believed that Ryan would probably do much better with an experienced teacher than with the average teaching assistant, who may only have a high school diploma. The disagreement with the teaching assistant was about Ryan perfecting his handwriting skills. The teaching assistant insisted that Ryan needed to write out all of his assignments in cursive in order to develop his skills. Because of Ryan's history of having great difficulty with writing, the teaching assistant's idea made no sense whatsoever. We called an IEP meeting to discuss the issue. At the meeting the teaching assistant argued that Ryan needed to learn to write well, because he would need to use this skill in the future. After he finished talking, Matt asked the new diagnostician what she was using to record the meeting. Of course, the question was rhetorical – everyone could see what she was using to accomplish this task. As the reader has undoubtedly guessed, it was a laptop computer. The question made the point that current technology – not to mention future technology – precludes the need for good handwriting skills. It would certainly be nice for Ryan to write well, but it would require a great deal of time and effort for him to learn, and there were many more important skills that he needed to learn. We were notified a few weeks after the meeting that the teaching assistant would be replaced. A new teaching assistant began working with Ryan the following week. DeAnn observed Ryan in the sixth-grade classroom for several days and was satisfied that he was doing well. We began checking junior high schools.

DeAnn had been to several junior high campuses through her work with the Parent Training and Information Center (PTI). We eliminated those schools where we thought we would have the most difficulty with the staff. The school DeAnn kept coming back to would require that Ryan receive a transfer in order to be able to register at the campus. DeAnn knew that the district was very strict about transfers, so she scheduled an appointment with the special education director and the special education coordinator. She explained her reasons for having Ryan attend this campus as opposed to the others. Fortunately they both agreed with her rationale. The coordinator and DeAnn made an appointment to meet the principal early in the spring. DeAnn liked him immediately. He seemed to be a straight shooter like the first elementary principal, and they also happened to be friends. DeAnn explained to the principal our reasons for wanting Ryan to attend his school.

She told him that we had heard very good things about his campus and knew that academics were stressed. By the end of the meeting the principal granted the transfer.

We were very concerned about how Ryan would adjust to junior high. Stories had been relayed to us about kids like Ryan being harassed mercilessly and about teachers who were focused on their own subject area and were resistant to making modifications for special education students. Another worry we had was the possibility of Ryan crossing paths with the vice-principals who are the disciplinarians of junior high campuses. Our major concern was that the support system that we had built over several years would be gone when Ryan left elementary school. We would have to start over again. The thought of having to expend the time and effort we knew would be necessary was overwhelming.

We talked with the special education director about our concerns, and she agreed to hire a particular psychologist from Houston whom DeAnn had met at a conference. DeAnn was impressed by her knowledge of Asperger Syndrome and agreed with her ideas about interventions. At their clinic the Houston psychologist and her husband, also a psychologist, worked primarily with children diagnosed with Asperger Syndrome and autism. Our plan was to have her assess Ryan's social skills level, make recommendations, and speak to the junior high staff who would be working with Ryan. The Houston psychologist asked that Ryan be given the WISC-III and a few other tests prior to her arrival. The new diagnostician at Ryan's school had taken an assessment class with Matt, so we knew that we had a competent evaluator. When she heard that she would be evaluating Ryan, she took a workshop on how to evaluate students with Asperger Syndrome. We felt her results accurately reflected Ryan's functioning level. A psychologist from the local education service center administered the parent questionnaires. DeAnn answered several questions with qualifiers because she was still rather wary of evaluators.

Two or three weeks later the Houston psychologist arrived to conduct her evaluation. After she had administered her testing, she sat down with us to discuss her findings. She expressed her concerns about Ryan's limited social skills. She stated that Ryan was far behind his peers. Matt commented that Ryan seemed to be unaware of the fact that he was quite different from his typical peers. The psychologist looked at Matt and stated, 'One day soon, he will. These kids are bright enough to figure out that they are different.' Although it was difficult to hear this from her, we knew she was right. Before she left to go back home, she gave us her draft of the evaluation report. Ryan finally received what we had long ago believed to be the correct diagnosis of Asperger Disorder.

We expected that there would be little communication between elementary and junior high staff about Ryan. We asked the special education director to arrange a meeting between the elementary school staff and the junior high staff. The junior high teachers would later comment on how helpful this meeting was for them. DeAnn, also, came up with the idea of developing a portfolio that would contain information about our family and Ryan's elementary school years. The final product included pictures with short descriptions, family history information, along with our hopes and dreams for the future, work samples, evaluation reports, and information on Asperger Syndrome. A major portion of the portfolio contained questionnaires that all of Ryan's teachers from second grade through sixth grade had completed. The questions were on how Ryan learned, how he interacted, how he made the transition from one activity to the next, and so on. On the last page of the questionnaire DeAnn asked the teachers to list what they had known about Asperger Syndrome/autism and their concerns prior to working with Ryan. Almost everyone wrote that they did not know how to work with a child like Ryan. DeAnn then asked what they had learned after working with him. We were amazed by the fact that almost all them stated what a pleasure their experience with Ryan had been, and they commented on how much they had learned. We were aware that they had all put a great deal of effort into working with Ryan. After reading what the teachers had written on the questionnaires, we realized how much they had grown to love Ryan as a person. DeAnn would later give a copy of the portfolio to the junior high principal to share with Ryan's new teachers.

Leaving the elementary school was very hard emotionally. We had formed friendships with many teachers and staff over the years. It was difficult to think of an appropriate going-away gift for the staff who had dedicated so much time and effort to Ryan. Finally Ryan and DeAnn came up with an idea for a gift that could only come from Ryan. Since third grade, Ryan had taken his lunch to school. Every day he brought a bacon sandwich. It became a joke in fifth grade for the teachers to hide his lunch from him. The whole class enjoyed the game. One morning DeAnn forgot to put Ryan's lunch in his backpack. Ryan and one of his friends had walked across the hall to the fourth-grade class to accuse the teacher of hiding his lunch. This time she was innocent. The night before the last day of school, Ryan and DeAnn made several bacon sandwiches and put them in separate lunch bags. The next morning they passed out bacon sandwiches to all of the teachers who had worked with Ryan. There was not a dry eye among the teachers after receiving their bacon sandwich.

What we learned

We experienced many changes during these years. One of the significant changes during Ryan's time in elementary school was the loss of a supportive principal after Ryan finished fourth grade.

Although one who proved to be unsympathetic replaced him, we continued to receive a great deal of support from campus staff. We learned the importance of developing good relationships with Ryan's teachers. Our experiences allowed us to be more effective participants in the IEP meetings. We continued to do our research and have discussions before making requests to the IEP committee. This practice helped us in several ways. It ensured that we had the law behind us, it helped us to be realistic about what we were advocating, and it allowed us to anticipate objections by committee members. These practices increased our chances of successfully advocating for Ryan. On the whole, the IEP meetings ran smoothly, even though the new principal was present.

Both of us learned an important lesson about evaluation during this time. We knew that Ryan had difficulties with reading. When the school district evaluated Ryan's reading, we were unaware that they were doing so to see whether he qualified for a reading program that was already in place. What should have happened is for a reading specialist to evaluate Ryan and determine his problem with reading. Then the IEP committee could have developed an individualized reading intervention plan through IEP goals and objectives. What happened instead is that Ryan was placed in a pre-existing program that did not address his specific reading needs. We still wonder what would have happened with Ryan's reading if he had been in an appropriate reading program.

Ryan continued to mature socially, but at a much slower pace than his classmates. As time passed, the separation between Ryan and his classmates became greater and greater. The dwindling number of children attending his birthday parties was evidence of this. When a boy whom Ryan considered his best friend hurt his feelings one day, we knew that a point had been reached when his peers were no longer willing to tolerate his peculiar way of interacting socially. The Houston psychologist's comment about Ryan being sharp enough to figure out that he was different would later prove to be true. Although we were well aware at this time that Ryan was experiencing major problems with social interactions, we were not sure about how to intervene effectively. This made us feel sad for Ryan, frustrated with not knowing how to 'fix' the problem, and discouraged about Ryan's future.

At the close of sixth grade, we began to prepare for Ryan's transition to junior high school. We knew that when Ryan left elementary school, he would be leaving a safe and protective environment. Ryan's safety had not been of concern to us in elementary school because everyone knew him and watched out for him. We were very concerned, however, about his safety in junior high school. We had heard several discouraging stories of kids like Ryan being picked on. We were expecting this kind of behavior towards Ryan and were determined to keep it to a minimum.

What you can do

- Become familiar with the rules regarding what information on your child is confidential and how the records are to be kept.

- Check into your options for a teaching assistant/paraprofessional.

- Learn the legal timelines that govern your child's education – for example; How much time does your campus have to administer evaluations? When is the Individual Education Program supposed to be implemented?

- Learn about educational evaluation.

- Provide the evaluator with information on your child's disorder.

- Ask questions on how the evaluator will evaluate your child.

- Become familiar with ways of helping your child during the evaluation (e.g., specifying breaks, time of day).

- Request that evaluation results be written in a descriptive format in the report; in other words, test scores should not just be listed, but instead written out in detail, specifying what the results of the tests mean. This will make the report more comprehensible both to educators and to parents.

- If evaluation results seem incorrect, then show the report to someone who is familiar with evaluation who can explain what the report means.

- Do not make your child's label the focus of the fight. Concentrate on supports, services, and interventions.

- If your child is having problems with reading, research and learn about various reading programs. Be sure that your child's reading is evaluated by a reading specialist to provide appropriate intervention.

- Investigate problems at school by talking to the staff; if necessary, visit the campus.

- Visit the school campus before your child attends.

- Prepare your child for transitions beforehand:
    - visit the new environment;
    - prepare the new staff for your child and provide information on his/her disability;
    - develop a portfolio giving information on how your child learns, providing work samples, and so on;
    - identify one key person your child can talk to when problems arise.

Chapter Five

Junior High School

Seventh grade — fall

The transition to junior high school began when Ryan went on his first tour of the school campus during the spring semester of sixth grade. Then, during the summer vacation, we received Ryan's schedule for seventh grade; it came about a week before the beginning of school, because we had requested that we receive it early. This allowed us to help Ryan find his new classrooms without all the noise and confusion that takes place on the first day of school. Students typically receive their class schedule on the first day of class, but this practice is hard for any typical seventh grader, let alone someone like Ryan. DeAnn and Ryan went up to the school and walked the halls until they had located all of his classrooms. Then they spent a few more days with Ryan practicing walking the route he would have to take getting from classroom to classroom. The principal suggested that Ryan help the staff set up classrooms for a few days before the school year began. This would allow him to become more familiar with the school and give him the opportunity to meet staff members, his new teachers, and some students. One of the teachers whom Ryan saw was the daughter of Ryan's second-grade teacher. He said that it was like having a part of his elementary school at junior high. He most enjoyed meeting some of the cheerleaders.

We knew that Ryan had an incredible memory, but we were worried that he would get lost on the first day of school, with all the commotion during hall passing time. It is common knowledge that most typical seventh-grade students are overwhelmed and lost on the first day. No one knew how Ryan would respond to a hall full of students moving from classroom to classroom. To help Ryan, the counselor had found a ninth-grade student who would help him navigate through the halls during the passing period on the first day of school. It was very difficult for DeAnn to watch Ryan leaving with the ninth grader, but difficult as it was, she knew that Ryan had to be successful – this was a make-it-or-break-it day. She went home to spend the day worrying about how Ryan was doing at school and thinking of everything that could go wrong. She waited for the phone to ring, but it never did. About ten minutes before dismissal time, DeAnn arrived at the school to wait for Ryan outside the counselor's office. The counselor, trying to contain her laughter, told DeAnn that at one point during the day the ninth grader had come to her office in a panic. He had lost Ryan. As it turned out, Ryan, tired of waiting for the ninth grader, just went to his next class without him. When they arrived at home, Ryan commented enthusiastically that he did not get lost once, but his friends did. We had successfully made it through the first day of junior high.

For two weeks, DeAnn went to the school and waited for Ryan outside the counselor's room. She was concerned about Ryan finding the car, because the campus was so large compared to the elementary school. After about two weeks, the counselor made it known that DeAnn was no longer welcome to sit outside her office to wait for Ryan. After rehearsing several times where DeAnn would park, Ryan was able to locate the car.

We had agreed to place Ryan in Resource Math, Resource Skills, and Resource Reading. It was a compromise for us, but we wanted to make sure that Ryan had the basic academic foundations in math, organization skills, and reading that he needed. It was not until about a month after school began that DeAnn became aware that the reading level of the resource class was much too low for Ryan. He was reading at a fifth-grade level, through his own hard work and the assistance of the elementary school staff and us. In 1994, when the Dallas psychologist had visited Ryan, he had been a non-reader, but by the beginning of seventh grade he was only two grade levels behind in his reading skills. The junior high school reading teacher was using material at a second- to third-grade level, which was much too low for Ryan. DeAnn asked the reading teacher if she could change the reading level for Ryan, but she was told that that was not possible. She then asked the teacher for an alternative to her class, and was told that Ryan could go into a regular reading class. DeAnn informed the counselor of her discussion with the reading teacher and the need to have Ryan placed in a regular reading class. The counselor spent much time rearranging Ryan's classes to fit him into the reading class. An Individual Education Plan (IEP) committee had to be convened to make the change official. A few days before the IEP meeting, when DeAnn asked the counselor if we needed to change the reading goals and objectives, she told DeAnn with a look of surprise that since Ryan was moving into a regular reading class, there would be no goals or objectives, as students in regular classes never have them. DeAnn pointed out that basically there were three steps to the special education process. First, the child is evaluated for services. If the child qualifies, IEP goals and objectives are developed, using the evaluation data. Then and only then does the IEP committee decide on the appropriate placement for a special education student. Goals and objectives never disappeared because of a placement. It was obvious to DeAnn from the look on the counselor's face that she did not appreciate getting a lesson on IEP development from a parent, but she had demonstrated that she did not even have a rudimentary knowledge of the special education process. We wondered how many other parents had been told the same thing, and what the impact was on their child's education. It seemed to be a common practice in our local school district to have the counselor with the least seniority and without the benefit of having a working knowledge of special education procedures assigned to special education students.

During the IEP meeting to ratify the change in placement, DeAnn encountered a great deal of resistance to the idea of modifying the goals and objectives. The reading goal stated that Ryan would make one year's progress in reading. She knew that the present goal and objectives were no longer appropriate for Ryan's new placement, but she chose not to push the issue at that time. She agreed to have them remain the same, with the stipulation that Ryan be assessed mid-way through the year. DeAnn's thinking was that this period would be sufficient to demonstrate that the reading goal and objectives were not appropriate.

Ryan was assigned to a speech therapist for junior high who was a good friend of Ryan's first speech therapist. We had heard that she was an excellent therapist with many years of experience, so we were excited about her working with Ryan. It was obvious from the beginning that she had strong opinions about how to work with kids, and she insisted upon doing her job in her own way. DeAnn suggested that she observe Ryan in his classroom environment and then work with him one-on-one in the speech room. She disagreed with our idea because she did not feel that that would be an effective way of conducting speech therapy. DeAnn also talked to her about enlisting peers as mentors who could facilitate Ryan's social interactions, but neither the therapist nor the principal was in agreement with this idea. When DeAnn brought up the idea at IEP meetings, they adamantly voiced their objections. The principal felt that this would make Ryan stand out, and the speech therapist felt that it would be a violation of Ryan's right to confidentiality.

In early October, the special education department notified us that a psychologist from Oklahoma would be visiting the district to evaluate some students with autism. They expressed an interest in having her also observe Ryan. We had met the psychologist a year earlier at a conference. We had been impressed with the presentation she gave, so we agreed to have her observe Ryan. After watching him, the psychologist, who demonstrated knowledge and competence in the area of high-functioning autism, stated that she was not very concerned about Ryan's social skills level and that he was doing fine. She then suggested that organizational skills development should be the focus of the school's efforts to teach Ryan. By the time Ryan reached sixth grade, we noticed a dramatic difference in his level of social maturity as compared to that of his peers. We embraced the hope contained in the words of the psychologist for only a few moments. Then we snapped back into reality. At the time, we decided not to object to her recommendation to focus on organizational skills. Ryan did need help with organizational skills, and we were happy that she pointed out this need to the educators. The IEP committee, on the other hand, had already recommended that Ryan be placed in resource skills in order to enhance his organizational skills, so we were all aware of this need. The question we were asking ourselves was why this autism specialist would say that Ryan was doing fine socially and we did not need to focus on social skills development. We left the meeting very confused by what she had told us.

Later in October, we were contacted by the Yale University Child Study Center. About a year earlier they had sent us a second set of questionnaires and a request for a videotape of Ryan, and we had returned the questionnaires, along with the requested videotape. We were told that Ryan was a candidate for the research project they were conducting. If we could arrange for travel to New Haven, they would evaluate Ryan. We made arrangements for all of us to fly out to Connecticut, and we arrived in New Haven the week before Thanksgiving.

Our expectation was that Ryan, alone, would be evaluated. Although we were told later that notice had been given, it was a surprise to learn that we would all be evaluated. Both of us had administered evaluations and intelligence tests to children as part of our graduate coursework, so it was an interesting and revealing experience to be the subjects this time. After three full days being evaluated, we were left feeling exhausted. Everyone at Yale was a pleasure to work with, and in spite of the grueling schedule we enjoyed the experience. At the end of the third day, we sat down with the researchers to discuss the results of Ryan's evaluation. DeAnn's greatest fear was that they would tell us that Ryan did not have Asperger Syndrome. As it turned out, her fears were unfounded. The evaluation results showed that Ryan clearly had Asperger Syndrome, and his most significant deficit area was in social skills. They were impressed with the interventions and supports that we had managed to obtain for Ryan. It seems that we made an impression on them, because we were invited to write an essay on how we developed from being parents to being parent/professionals for their upcoming book, *Asperger Syndrome*. They also asked DeAnn to come back and make a presentation at their conference the following spring.

Our trip to Yale validated our thinking and the interventions we had been pushing for for years. We had believed for quite some time that Ryan had Asperger Syndrome with average intelligence, and the Yale researchers confirmed this. We had also been advocating a focus on social skills development, which, in our minds, superseded academics. Again, we heard from one of the foremost researchers in the United States and probably worldwide that the most critical area requiring intervention was in the social realm. The researcher basically said that Ryan demonstrated the capacity to learn academic subjects, and he had a lifetime to do so. On the other hand, he was struggling socially, and he had a limited window of opportunity when it came to social skills development.

In spite of the limited availability of information on Asperger Syndrome and the local professionals who did not agree that Ryan had Asperger Syndrome, we had pushed hard for those supports and services that seemed appropriate for someone with Asperger Syndrome. For the most part we had relied on our intuition as our guide in pushing for certain interventions, and for the most part we had been on the mark. It is hard to say what we would have done differently if we had not received what we believe to be a definitive diagnosis from the group of researchers who did the field trials for the DSM-IV diagnosis. We do know that we would not have given in to the pressures of provincial wisdom.

When we returned home, DeAnn pushed the speech therapist harder about working with Ryan with typical peers rather than just one-on-one. They had several meetings, each more heated. DeAnn's plan made so much sense to us that we failed to understand the reason for resistance. At one meeting, the therapist informed DeAnn that she was the speech expert; DeAnn returned fire by saying that she was Ryan's mother and had expertise in numerous aspects of his functioning, not just one. We both decided to attend the next meeting around the end of the semester because DeAnn and the speech teacher had reached an impasse. We are not sure whether she was persuaded by the logic of Matt's argument, the passion with which he asserted it, or a combination of the two, but the speech teacher agreed at that meeting to try the things that we had suggested. Plans were then made for the following year.

It was at around this time that we began having a difficult time with Ryan's teaching assistant who let DeAnn know how upset and angry she was about our not requiring Ryan to do all of his homework. We decided that because Ryan really liked her, we would let it pass. Mistakenly, we thought that the matter had been dealt with at the transition IEP meeting when Ryan was leaving elementary school. At that meeting, the counselor had informed DeAnn that Ryan would be having a great deal more homework than in elementary school. DeAnn told the counselor that we had not allowed any homework for Ryan during elementary school. She explained that Ryan's school day had already been extended by therapies and, for a couple of years, by the reading program, so we decided to eliminate homework. The counselor then told DeAnn that there *would* be homework in junior high. DeAnn conveyed our position on homework by saying that when Ryan is given 'homework,' it is we, the parents, who are expected to see that it is completed, and therefore we would decide how much homework Ryan would complete. We felt that Ryan had a hard enough time getting through the school day, let alone having to contend with homework. When we saw that he was becoming overwhelmed, we allowed him to stop. Later on we required him to spend only an hour on his homework; after that, we let him decide whether to continue or to stop. More often than not he would continue for a while longer, and sometimes until he finished. The IEP committee had also agreed that Ryan would have time available to him in resource skills to do homework.

During the school year, from time to time Ryan would tell us about things that had happened with the teaching assistant. According to Ryan, on at least a few occasions one of his teachers had pulled the teaching assistant out into the hall to tell her to calm down. Fortunately, at the end of seventh grade the teaching assistant decided to leave of her own accord.

Seventh grade – spring

The month of January was over, and the school had not administered a reading evaluation. When DeAnn reminded the counselor of the IEP committee agreement, the counselor made the necessary arrangements to begin the evaluation. In early February she showed DeAnn the results of two different reading evaluations. One showed that Ryan's reading level had dropped. This was the same evaluation tool that had been administered the year before. Another evaluation showed he had not made any progress. The counselor said that it was not that Ryan had lost ground; he just had not made any progress. She explained that many seventh graders did not read as well as Ryan did. The more the counselor talked, the more concerned DeAnn became. She had taken several evaluation classes and had written a book for parents on educational evaluation. She knew very well what the results of the testing were saying. Ryan had lost ground in reading. We had worked too hard to get him to the reading level he had reached just to accept casually Ryan's current reading level.

When DeAnn got home, she called the elementary school and talked to Ryan's elementary school teachers. She asked them what they recommended to help with Ryan's reading. DeAnn learned from the content mastery teacher that one of the first-grade teachers also tutored children using the Spalding method of reading. The teacher agreed to tutor Ryan when DeAnn made the necessary arrangements. DeAnn called the counselor and began telling her how successfully the elementary school had worked with Ryan. The counselor was very clear that she did not appreciate DeAnn talking to the elementary school staff. DeAnn, on the other hand, was clear about how disappointed we were about the junior high school's lack of success with Ryan's reading. The counselor and DeAnn agreed that DeAnn would continue talking to the elementary school staff and sharing the information with the junior high staff.

We had an IEP meeting and set up the tutoring. Fortunately, DeAnn had a copy of the goals and objectives that stated that Ryan would make a year of progress in reading. She also knew Ryan's reading level. The information was necessary to establish the fact that Ryan had lost ground in his reading. This paved the way to advocate successfully for tutoring. It was a valuable lesson for us regarding evaluations. Ryan received tutoring on the weekends for the remainder of the school year, and five days a week during the summer. Ryan's decoding skills improved by four grade levels. Reading comprehension was the area to watch now.

At the end of seventh grade, we had our annual IEP meeting. DeAnn informed the IEP committee that she planned to test Ryan's reading level. To our dismay, we again had on our junior high IEP team the original diagnostician from elementary school – the same person who had told us to let educators do their job and who refused to lock the file cabinet. In every IEP meeting she and DeAnn managed to get into an argument about evaluation, and this meeting was no different. The diagnostician finally agreed to DeAnn administering the reading evaluation. The diagnostician and the counselor then announced that the meeting needed to end because they had another family waiting. Although we felt that they rushed us through the end of the meeting, we signed the paperwork. We felt that a sufficient number of issues had been addressed and interventions written into the IEP. We also knew that we could call another IEP meeting to cover what we had not addressed in this one. We had not experienced being rushed through an IEP meeting in quite a long time, and we left with an uneasy feeling, but aware that this experience is not uncommon for many parents. We decided that we would request an IEP meeting at the beginning of the following year to finish discussing what we felt needed to be discussed.

One of the cheerleaders who had taken Ryan under her wing left junior high to go on to high school. He had really enjoyed her friendship, and he was left feeling very upset. Ryan had told DeAnn about a girl in his craft class who was friendly to him. We arranged for Ryan and this young lady to take tennis lessons together during the summer. DeAnn met her parents and really liked them both. Sometime in late July, Ryan's tennis partner went to the East Coast with her family to visit relatives, and Ryan and DeAnn went to Dallas to visit his grandparents; we never managed to arrange for Ryan and the young lady to get together during the remainder of the summer.

Eighth grade – fall

Before the new school year began, DeAnn and Ryan again went to the school to locate Ryan's new classrooms and to help teachers prepare their classrooms. As in years past, DeAnn asked each new teacher whether they had any questions about Ryan and Asperger Syndrome. Three of the four new teachers did not know that Ryan had Asperger Syndrome, nor did they know anything about the disorder. The fourth teacher recognized Ryan from seventh grade and had asked another teacher about him. DeAnn was alarmed, as this was the first time that the teachers had not been given information about Ryan and his learning issues since he had started school in West Texas. DeAnn immediately called the special education director and the principal to inform them of the situation and the fact that we were very upset about it. Ryan's math teacher, who had taken a special interest in Ryan, provided a quick in-service seminar for the new teachers.

A few weeks after school began, we requested an IEP meeting to discuss the teachers not having been informed about Ryan, along with a new disturbing development taking place in the cafeteria. We thought we would also discuss issues that had been left at the spring meeting because we were rushed. The first concern we discussed was the fact that no one had talked to the new teachers about Ryan. We acknowledged partial responsibility for the problem, since we had failed to establish who would talk to the new teachers. The counselor said that they liked the new teachers to experience the student first, and then tell them about a student's disorder. The look on our faces must have expressed what we were thinking, because she did not discuss the matter any further. We had purchased a Tony Attwood video tape titled *Asperger Syndrome: A video for parents and professionals.* The tape provided an overview of Asperger Syndrome and information on various inverventions. DeAnn requested that all the teachers watch at least the first half of the three hours. DeAnn would later go round to each of Ryan's teachers to see whether they had any questions about the tape. We also persuaded the district to arrange a phone consultation for Ryan's IEP team with an autism expert, Carol Gray. We had met her for the first time at the Yale conference. We had attended her workshop at the Region Service Center and had had dinner with her only a few months before. Since she knew Ryan and had extensive knowledge and experience of autism, we were confident that her input would be greatly beneficial and appreciated by the school staff. We then asked who would be responsible for talking to the ninth-grade teachers the following year. The principal said he would talk to them about Ryan.

The next issue we discussed was the problem occurring in the cafeteria. It had started the first week of school. Ryan decided to sit with the girl with whom he had played tennis during the summer. On the first Friday of the school year, Ryan reported that some girls were pulling his chair out from under him at lunch. It really hurt his feelings. We decided to see whether Ryan could handle the situation on his own. Every day, Ryan came home with a new story about the girls in the lunchroom. They would trick him into moving, or, if he refused to move, they would pull his chair out from under him. For several nights we sat down with Ryan and talked about his being teased. We asked him what the girl he wanted to sit next to did when he was being forced to move. He said that she did nothing. We asked Ryan whether other boys sat at the table with the girls. He told us, 'no.' We gave him several suggestions on what he could say to handle the situation. He continued to come home with more stories. After two weeks, we suggested that he should move to the table where his friends sat. In the morning, before he went to school, DeAnn asked Ryan what he had decided. Ryan said that he would try the girls one more time. DeAnn told him that she thought he was a glutton for punishment, but it was his decision. That night he told us that he had changed his mind, and he sat with his friends. The two of us talked to the principal, even though it seemed that Ryan had taken care of his problem. DeAnn had watched her brother go through hell with teasing, and as a result she had a very low tolerance for that kind of behavior. DeAnn informed the principal that if he did not take care of the situation, we would. He said he would monitor what was happening with Ryan in the lunchroom. Both of us had many discussions with Ryan about his summer tennis partner. Ryan had continued to make overtures toward her, to no avail. It took us several months to convince Ryan that she was no longer interested in being his friend.

We then talked about those issues that had not been fully discussed during the previous IEP meeting. The meeting ended up lasting over five hours. At one point, DeAnn asked the principal whether he would like to adjourn the meeting. He said he wanted to complete the agenda. We could tell that the length of the meeting was wearing on him and the others. He exercised patience throughout the meeting, as did all of his staff, save one. They demonstrated true professionalism that is to be admired.

Ryan's new teaching assistant was a dream come true. She was calm and patient. She had a good sense of when to push Ryan and when to step back. The new teaching assistant and the speech therapist came up with a data collection method to keep track of how Ryan was interacting with his peers in various settings. They worked together on his social skills. From the very beginning, Ryan was comfortable with the new teaching assistant, and so were we.

Once again, we were fortunate in having good teachers at this campus. His math teacher, in particular, took to Ryan. It turned out that the teacher was the best friend of a friend of DeAnn's and she spoke with DeAnn on a regular basis about Ryan and Asperger Syndrome. She became the campus coordinator for Ryan's IEP, and she talked with all of the teachers to make sure Ryan was doing well. Although she could be strict and provided a very structured environment, she was light-hearted and always laughing. The students, including Ryan, were very comfortable with her. One evening, when he had several homework assignments, DeAnn asked Ryan what he was going to work on first. He gave her a puzzled look and said, 'Why, math, of course. She is too good a teacher to not put first.' When DeAnn conveyed this story to the teacher at an IEP meeting, she blushed with pride; she commented that she thought a lot of Ryan.

Early in the fall semester, the special education director called to let us know that it was time for Ryan's three-year evaluation. She asked whether the associate psychologist could compile the results of the Yale report and several others into one. She said that she could find someone else, but she really thought that he would be the best person for the job. We thought through the evaluation in third grade. After five years, DeAnn still became upset thinking about it. The director told DeAnn that if we did not like the results, she would get someone else to compile the report. We thought about the length of time that had passed, and we wondered whether it was fair not to give this person the opportunity. DeAnn told the director that we felt that it was time to let go of the past, and we gave our consent.

The associate psychologist faxed us his report after receiving additional information from us. The report turned out to be very good – one of the best reports we had seen. We were pleasantly surprised. The associate psychologist went to Ryan's school to show them his recommendations. Apparently, the meeting with the school staff did not go very well. They had not been very open to his suggestions. When he communicated to us the discussion he had had with the school staff, DeAnn recognized who had said what. His final report was strongly worded, and it accurately represented Ryan and his needs. It helped us to get more supports for Ryan. During our last phone conversation, DeAnn told the psychologist that she felt he had really come through for Ryan, and that she was through being angry with him. He laughed and said that he had always tried to do what was best for Ryan. DeAnn wrote a letter to the director, telling her what a fine job he had done. Though the associate psychologist and we still have our disagreements on issues, we feel that we have come to a point in time where we can let bygones be bygones.

The principal had recommended on several occasions that Ryan should attend ball games; he told us that he and the vice-principal would keep an eye on Ryan. We were unwilling to let Ryan attend these games, partly because he did not like ball sports and partly because we knew that Ryan did not have the social skills to benefit from being turned loose at a ball game without an adult tutoring him. To us, it seemed like setting Ryan up for a social fiasco. After several conversations with the principal, it was clear to both of us that he felt that if we just placed Ryan in a typical social environment, he would acquire the necessary social skills. It was obvious that the principal had the best of intentions, but clearly he did not understand the implications of Ryan's disorder.

Eighth grade – spring

By this time, Ryan had been in junior high for a year and a half. The junior high school staff expressed that he was doing just fine academically – better than many other students. The staff working with Ryan continued to provide indications that they really did not have a sense of what Ryan's challenges were socially. The idea that Ryan was like other students did not include the way in which he operated socially. At almost every IEP meeting the principal and counselor would take the opportunity to make statements about their witnessing Ryan interacting with other students. They would comment how they would watch Ryan in the halls, and he acted like every other junior high student. As much as we wanted Ryan to be like the other students, we knew he was not. By the way that they talked, it seemed that they truly believed what they were saying. We were becoming very irritated with their stories about Ryan. To us, his social difficulties were so apparent, that even the casual observer would notice. These people had known Ryan for a year and a half, so we had some idea why they were telling us that Ryan acted like a typical eigth grader. We had continued to push for peer mentoring, and we were met with opposition. As a result of this, and of Ryan's glaringly obvious social difficulties, we began to believe that they were saying things about Ryan looking normal as a way of excusing them from providing some of the supports we had asked for. We believed that if this attitude continued, it would become more and more difficult to get Ryan the additional support he so desperately needed.

In Texas, we have an accountability system for all students, called the Texas Academic Achievement System (TAAS); all students are required to take this unless the IEP committee feels that a student receiving special education would not benefit from taking the TAAS. The result is that the IEP committee can exempt students who qualify for special education from the TAAS. At the time, students who were exempt from the TAAS did not receive scores that might pull down the overall campus scores. This was particularly appealing to principals, since by removing some of the lower-functioning students and keeping gifted and talented student scores, the campus TAAS scores would be higher, and raises and promotions are based on the TAAS scores. Ryan was exempt from taking TAAS.

During one IEP meeting, DeAnn was prepared for the principal and counselor to say once again that Ryan was like all the other eighth-grade students. When the principal made a statement to that effect, DeAnn said, 'Good, then he can take the TAAS.' The principal became very uneasy. He proceeded to show us some of Ryan's test scores, and he explained that Ryan would not benefit from the taking the TAAS. After his lengthy explanation, DeAnn looked at him and stated, 'Then what you are telling me is that Ryan is not like all the other eighth graders.' If the principal allowed Ryan to take the TAAS, in his mind he ran the risk of Ryan pulling down his campus scores; if he did not let Ryan take the TAAS, then he had to concede that DeAnn was correct. Neither he nor any other staff member ever made another comment about Ryan acting like a typical student.

In spite of the rough beginning, Ryan's eighth-grade year went extremely well. The speech therapist and the teaching assistant had come up with a great plan for working with Ryan on his social skills. The speech therapist would observe Ryan in his craft class once a week and work with him one-on-one in her therapy room. At one point, she told DeAnn how excited she was about Ryan's progress. She had rarely seen a student make so much progress so quickly. We were extremely pleased that we were all finally on the same page. Our relationship had gone from being a very tense one to a very comfortable one. We each respected the others' knowledge and expertise. Due to poor health, the speech therapist had to retire at the end of Ryan's eighth-grade year. We were saddened by the condition of her health, and we really hated losing her. She had invested a great deal of time and effort in helping Ryan, and his progress was readily apparent.

We had Ryan's end-of-year IEP meeting. The evaluation reports for math and reading, which had recently been completed, showed that Ryan had made a year's progress. We were very pleased with his progress, and we shared our joy with the school staff. We remarked on how quickly time had flown: in a few months, Ryan would be starting his final year in junior high. The committee discussed how much Ryan had matured since his first days there. While we were going over the IEP goals that we had developed for ninth grade, it occurred to us that we had a pretty good team.

Ninth grade - fall

DeAnn and Ryan again followed the well-established routine of visiting the school campus a short while before the first day of classes. We talked to the new teachers, and this time they had been briefed about Ryan and Asperger Syndrome. DeAnn asked the principal if he would like to borrow the Tony Attwood tape for the new teachers to view. He replied in the affirmative, and we were off to a great start.

In October, we received Ryan's first progress report. Receiving a progress report means that the student is not doing well in a particular class. This report was in science. We knew that science would be extremely difficult for Ryan, because in ninth grade it covered chemistry and physics. As a result of Ryan's difficulties in math, the IEP committee had decided not to place him in ninth-grade algebra. Both chemistry and physics required algebra, and we had been told by one teacher that most ninth graders struggle with this class. We had met the science teacher and really liked her.

DeAnn panicked and requested an IEP meeting, but she agreed to have an informal meeting with the principal and the science teacher in his office before having an IEP meeting. The teacher showed DeAnn her grade book and pointed out that Ryan had taken several tests. As he had not done very well the first time in taking the test, she allowed him to take an alternative test in the library, accompanied by the teaching assistant, who asked Ryan the test questions, and he wrote down the answers. On the retest in the library, which was a different test, Ryan did extremely well. The two grades would be averaged. Ryan was actually passing the class and had a 'B' average. We had received the progress report because it had been generated before Ryan's retest had been recorded on the school computer. The teacher said that Ryan always opted to take the first test in the classroom with all the other students, and she asked DeAnn whether she would prefer that he take the first test in the library. DeAnn replied that it was Ryan's decision as to whether he took the first test in class or in the library, because he needed to learn to make accommodations and modifications for himself. We were impressed with Ryan for having made the decision to take the tests in his classroom.

We found ourselves having to address the issue of homework again in ninth grade. We realized that homework would develop skills that Ryan needed to develop for his adult life, such as organizational skills and discipline. We had discussed homework at several IEP meetings. During seventh and eighth grade, we had limited the homework to an hour each evening, unless we felt that Ryan was capable of doing more. The IEP committee also scheduled time during the school day for Ryan to work on homework. We felt that Ryan had enough to contend with socially throughout the school day. By the time he came home, he was adamant about satisfying his need for what he referred to as 'down-time,' and we agreed. Our resistance to having Ryan complete all of his homework seemed to frustrate the educators, but they did work with us. During ninth grade, Ryan brought more homework home, especially at the end of each grading period. He became very frustrated on several occasions, so we instructed him to stop working and sent a note to the teachers. The IEP committee agreed to extended time as a modification which meant that Ryan had additional time to complete his school work and he would not be penalised for turning in late assignments. We occasionally found ourselves taking advantage of this intervention. One evening Ryan came home with more homework than we had ever seen. He was very upset, and so were we. Ryan pulled out a homework schedule that his resource teacher had compiled. She had taken the time to write out each subject and how much time Ryan needed to spend on it. She even scheduled in breaks. It worked like a charm. Ryan was less pressured, and he commented afterwards how much the schedule had helped him. A few days later DeAnn talked to his teacher and thanked her. She was delighted to hear the positive feedback. She and Ryan came up with a plan: at the end of each school day, they would write out his homework schedule. This helped a great deal by giving Ryan a set pattern to follow, with periodic breaks, which allowed him to do more homework without his feeling as overwhelmed as he had in the past. We maintained our stipulation that Ryan would only be required to do one hour of homework, but he would typically exceed this requirement, and quite often he finished all of his homework. We attribute his success primarily to the efforts of Ryan's resource teacher.

One day, when DeAnn went into the lunchroom to pick Ryan up for an orthodontist appointment, her heart sank. From the beginning of the school year, when Ryan's best friend had moved, a consultant had been assigned to check on Ryan from time to time during lunchroom time. Campus staff, the consultant, and Ryan had all assured us that the lunchroom time was just fine. What DeAnn saw was not 'just fine.' Ryan was sitting between two groups of students, with empty chairs to his right and across from him. It was obvious that he was eating lunch by himself. When DeAnn asked his teacher, she was told that the school staff had been watching him, and that he did interact with the others. DeAnn pointed out that sitting in close proximity and interacting were not the same thing.

On Friday of the same week, when DeAnn went to get Ryan from school, he was unusually late getting out of the building. After waiting for fifteen minutes, she finally went to his classroom. Ryan was not in the room, but his math teacher was there. She told DeAnn that Ryan had just left. She then went on to explain that she and the teaching assistant had had to talk to Ryan about following a particular girl all day. Ryan and DeAnn had seen the girl the evening before, at the grocery store. She had said hello to Ryan, and he asked her how she knew him. She told him that they had lockers next to each other. Although she was only fourteen, she had a special permit enabling her to drive by herself within the county limits. State law, however, did not allow her to drive to the grocery store by herself. As the legal driving age for most people is sixteen, her being able to drive at fourteen fascinated Ryan. The following day the girl had complained to a general education teacher that Ryan was following her, and it scared her. The general education teacher relayed this to Ryan's teacher, and she and the teaching assistant then talked to Ryan. The teacher told DeAnn that they had also talked to the girl and had explained Ryan's situation to her, and as a result the girl was no longer frightened about what had occurred. When the teacher finished relaying the story, DeAnn saw Ryan just outside the school doors. She could tell that he was close to tears, so they immediately left the campus. Some forty-five minutes passed before Ryan was able to state his version of what happened.

Ryan told us that he happened to see this girl in the hall after homeroom, and again after lunch. He said his interest in talking to her was: 'One, she was a girl, and two, I was fascinated by her driving.' In addition to having adjoining lockers, they had the same homeroom and lunch period. He said that he did not realize that he was following her. The teachers told Ryan that the girl might have told him off or slapped him, because she felt threatened. She also might have told her boyfriend or her father, the deputy sheriff. Ryan said that he believed that his teachers were trying to protect him when they told him those things. He had been thinking, 'How am I going to correct this mistake?', when the dismissal bell rang. When Ryan was walking down the hall after leaving his last class, he saw a girl whom he had known for several years. He said that, 'I talked to another girl, hoping I would get it right this time.' He then saw his teaching assistant walking down the hall in his direction. At that moment he was thinking, 'Maybe if I get it right, she will not mess with me.' Ryan tried to explain himself, but the teachers again chastised Ryan for his behavior. The teaching assistant told Ryan that the reason he was following the girls was because he did not care how they felt. This brought him to tears. He told us, 'They misread me.' Later that evening Ryan said to DeAnn, 'You know, Mom, instead of over-criticizing me, they should have told me what to do different.' It was apparent to us that he had not been following the girl. It was also obvious that Ryan was truly at a loss as to what he had done wrong.

Together, we explained what had probably happened with the first girl, and we suggested that he wait until girls approach him. We talked about the fact that he did nothing wrong with the second girl; it was just bad timing, because his teachers had just scolded him. Ryan told us that because of what had occurred, he would not interact with girls any more. This saddened us deeply, because this would reduce his opportunity to interact with his peers by about 50 percent.

After discussing the day's events, we decided that Ryan would not return to school until we had had a conversation with his teacher and teaching assistant. We were extremely angry about Ryan being told that he did not care about the girls' feelings and also because having talked at IEP meetings about interventions that were critically needed to support Ryan in social situations, we felt that we had encountered roadblock after roadblock from the other IEP committee members.

The following Monday we spoke with the teacher and teaching assistant. We told them that we had discussed our concerns about Ryan's social skills deficits time after time, only to be told by staff that he was doing fine, but what had occurred the preceding week clearly demonstrated that he was not 'doing fine.

The following day, we did let Ryan return to school. He seemed to have recovered from the situation much better than his parents. DeAnn called the special education director and told her what had happened, and requested that she attend an IEP meeting. The director agreed to attend and bring the associate psychologist.

She also requested that the parent liaison and speech therapist attend. We began preparing for the meeting.

Ninth grade - spring

The IEP meeting was scheduled for a Thursday afternoon a couple of weeks after the spring semester began. DeAnn attended the meeting by herself; Matt felt that they simply did not understand Ryan, and it would be futile at this point to make any further attempts to instruct them. There were several new faces at this meeting. The special education director had brought several different professionals with her, two of them from a program called 'Natural Helpers.' It was decided that Ryan would begin the Natural Helpers program immediately. This program identified student leaders on the campus and taught them skills to help other students. The lunchroom professional offered to start a music club at lunchtime to help promote friendships for Ryan. The associate psychologist offered to develop a method of tracking Ryan's interactions with other students during unstructured times. The special education director informed the junior high school staff how far Ryan had come: she described how he had come from a self-contained classroom and how successful he had been in the general education classroom. The committee agreed to implement a number of interventions at that meeting. However, DeAnn left with the expectation that it was very unlikely that there would be much follow-through.

Three months after the incident with the girl, we attended a conference on Nonverbal Learning Disabilities in San Antonio. The hosts allowed Ryan to participate in the conference. We heard Dr. Byron Rourke, Sue Thompson, and Dr. Loomis discuss various interventions for students with Nonverbal Learning Disabilities. For the most part, Ryan was able to sit and listen. During the long drive home, Ryan made a statement that surprised us. He said, 'You know, the junior high people are not working with me like they should be. I don't feel they are helping me.' We knew at this point that it was time to evaluate where all this was headed. We could no longer ignore that it was time to make some major changes in what we were doing with Ryan educationally.

When we returned home to West Texas, we began to discuss and explore options for Ryan's education. We came up with three options: continue with public school, enroll him in private school, or teach him ourselves through homeschool. To continue with public school was certainly an option. Realistically, we knew that we would have to push for teacher training and monitor the school personnel to ensure follow-through. The amount of our time that would be required of us to participate in Ryan's high school education based on our past experience would be staggering. Private schools generally have smaller classrooms; however, neither of us felt comfortable having Ryan attend any of the private schools located in our area. Our experience working with other families with children in private school told us that generally they were not inclined to working with students with special needs. We were also aware that we would not have any legal recourse to force a private school to make accommodations for Ryan. DeAnn began to research the option of homeschooling Ryan.

As the school semester continued, Ryan became more anxious and sometimes frantic about his homework. Because of this, we did not force him to complete assignments that came home. We felt that we had discussed this problem enough for the junior high school staff to know our position. One afternoon Ryan left school very upset, because his English teacher had told him that he was failing. When DeAnn picked Ryan up from school that day, she listened while Ryan raged about the failing English grade. Ryan had been told that he had low grades because he had not turned in his homework assignments. DeAnn initially thought that she could calm him down by talking to him, but Ryan was too upset. DeAnn decided to go to speak with the English teacher immediately. Two days later there was a call from the science teacher, stating that Ryan was not turning in assignments. DeAnn asked the science teacher the same question she had asked the English teacher: 'How does a child with a teaching assistant have so much trouble getting his assignments turned in?' The science teacher said that she would check into this and let DeAnn know if there was a problem. We did not hear from the science teacher again, but Ryan's level of stress with school continued to mount. Even though he had a class period each day to complete his homework, he still continued to bring home one or two hours' worth of homework almost every night, but we continued to allow Ryan to determine when he had done enough homework.

We had made it a habit to have Ryan accompany us on our business trips. In the past, we had mostly traveled during the summer months, so there was no conflict with school. During Ryan's ninth-grade school year we found ourselves traveling more often than we had in the past, and many of the places we went to provided a wonderful learning experience for Ryan. After arriving home from our Christmas vacation, we came to the conclusion that we could not leave Ryan in town with friends when we both had to travel. It was the incident where Ryan was accused of following the girl that prompted this thinking. We were not about to leave Ryan behind, with the possibility of another traumatic event occurring at school.

It had been a bad flu year, and as a result Ryan missed several days of school due to illness. After one of our trips, we were notified that we had been summoned to a meeting with the attendance officer. As it turned out, the meeting was with the attendance officer and the vice-principal. When we arrived, the vice-principal asked where Ryan was. DeAnn replied, ' I hope he is in school. Why, is there something you need to tell us?' The vice-principal said that the notice had stated that Ryan was to attend. Matt informed him that we did not think it was appropriate for Ryan to attend the meeting. He continued by saying that we were responsible for deciding when Ryan would be absent. Needless to say, this did not go over very well and set the tone for the meeting. They proceeded to tell us about Ryan's absences. We discussed the number of times he had been sick and the number of times he had come on trips with us. All the trips had been excused absences. The vice-principal commented that Ryan's low grades resulted from his absences. We asked how this could be, when we always requested make-up work, which was always completed and turned in upon his return. The vice-principal had no answer. He then read documents from both the English teacher and the science teacher about Ryan's grades. DeAnn replied that she had talked to the teachers about Ryan's grades, and both teachers had assured DeAnn that the problems had already been taken care of. When we were cautioned about any further absences, we informed the attendance officer that we would be taking another trip in about a month, that Ryan would be going with us, and that he would be absent for three days. At the end of the meeting we pointed that as Ryan was a student receiving special education services, the meeting had been inappropriate. Legally, they were required to request an IEP meeting first, to establish whether there was a correlation between Ryan's absences and his disability. DeAnn then wrote, requesting a meeting to discuss Ryan's attendance, low grades, and the teaching assistant.

During the meeting it was discussed that Ryan was not failing and that the district tended to exaggerate low grades at these meetings in order to alarm the parents and to encourage attendance. The missing school work was discussed, and it was determined that school staff would be responsible for identifying why the work was not being turned in and making sure that it was handed in on time. DeAnn brought up the fact that Ryan was experiencing a great deal of stress over homework. The IEP committee developed methods to limit the homework. Again, we left the meeting with the feeling that there would be limited follow-through. A few weeks later Ryan received another progress report for two classes because of work not being turned in.

One day about a month before the end of the school year, Ryan informed us that he was being teased. It was happening during one of his classes, with the teacher present. We are confident that the teacher was unaware of the teasing, because she would have put a stop to it immediately. The teasing continued for a short time in the hall after class. That evening Matt gave Ryan some suggestions on how to respond if he encountered any further problems with the boys who were teasing him. Fortunately, the next day at school nothing happened. What was upsetting for us about the situation was that for the first time the teasing registered with Ryan, and he was frightened about going back to school.

For the three years he had attended junior high, Ryan had been involved in a program for gifted and talented students. Each year the team of students had to solve a problem in a creative way and present the solution at a competition. This year the program involved the students developing a script, making their own costumes, and building a set. The group won the regional competition, which meant that Ryan had the opportunity to go to the state championship in Dallas with his group and several others. We were very comfortable with Ryan's coach. She had been Ryan's seventh-grade teacher, and she had been involved with him for two-and-a-half years. We also noticed that Ryan's team members were very accepting of him, so we decided that Ryan was ready and in capable hands; we allowed him to join them on the chartered bus and to stay with them in the hotel. We drove to Dallas and stayed with family. The hotel Ryan was staying in turned out to be located only a couple of miles from where we were staying. Ryan had a wonderful time with his team, and we feel he benefited greatly from the experience.

At the end of the school year another IEP meeting was scheduled to discuss plans for Ryan's transition to high school. DeAnn had attended an IEP meeting for a friend at the high school, so she had had an opportunity to meet the school staff and to see the school, which had a very good reputation in the community. The director of special education had offered to have Ryan participate in a pilot program at a different high school in the district. It was a general education initiative, which meant that general education teachers would be taught how to work with students with different learning styles. Only three high schools in the United States had been chosen, and one of these was in our city. It sounded very promising, but upon closer inspection we became concerned about the length of time it would take to train staff to a point that would be helpful for Ryan. There were several private schools in our area as well. The time to make the decision was fast approaching – we had to reach a decision soon about where Ryan would be receiving his education in the future.

We knew that with Ryan beginning school on another campus, we would once again have to see that the school staff received training on Asperger Syndrome, in addition to visiting the campus on a regular basis to make sure that the IEP was followed. Our concern about Ryan being teased was another worry for us. Ryan would be an easy target in high school, and we worried about the impact it would have on his self-esteem. We did not relish the thought of expending so much energy ensuring that Ryan received what he needed, and we wondered whether it would be worth it. Finally, we made our decision.

What we learned

Ryan attending junior high school brought with it many new challenges. One of the major challenges we encountered was making sure that the educators followed through on what had been agreed upon at meetings. Our attempts to put in place interventions that would contribute to Ryan's social as well as his academic development were met with a great deal of opposition. We believe that the resistance came primarily from two sources: the mind-set of the educators when it came to working with someone like Ryan, and the education system. Battling these combined forces required the participation of both of us. With certain issues we found ourselves gaining ground, only to lose it the following year, or sometimes within the same school year. We continually had to revisit issues that we thought had been resolved. This was especially frustrating, and it consumed a great deal of energy. We had learned during our many years of working with educators that in order to build and maintain a cooperative spirit, it was necessary to conduct ourselves in a professional manner. Successfully advocating for Ryan also required that we had knowledge in a variety of areas, including Asperger Syndrome, education law, and teaching strategies for academics and social skills. Our knowledge and experience is probably greater than that of most parents – at least, anyone we know. On several occasions we found that it was simply not enough to be knowledgeable and experienced during the junior high years. As parents, we did not have the power to make the educators do what we knew to be necessary and appropriate for Ryan. There were too many people we had to work with, and this was therefore very time-consuming to manage. We were also contending with a system that was strongly biased toward the education of typical students, which precluded to a great extent the implementation of a truly individualized education program for our son. The time had come to look to the future and to decide whether to continue spending our time and energy on forcing the public school system to educate our son as required by federal law, or to explore other educational opportunities.

What you can do

- Prepare for transition to junior high school early in the spring of the preceding school year.

- Take your child on a tour of the school building before the start of the school year.

- Get your child's class schedule before the beginning of the school year. Walk the schedule with your child until he/she has the route memorized.

- Have your child meet his/her teachers before the first day of school.

- Have your child work on campus before the beginning of the school year; this allows your child to become familiar with the campus staff and other children and gives an opportunity for the campus staff to become familiar with your child.

- Ask the teacher if he/she has been informed of your child and his/her disorder.

- Appoint one person on the campus to be responsible for informing new staff on your child and his/her disorder; check with that person before the start of the year to make sure members of staff have been informed.

- Have the campus appoint a peer for the first week of school to help your child find his/her way to classes.

- Make sure that one staff member on campus is responsible for coordinating with the other teachers and for all aspects of your child's school day.

- Have the principal get to know your child. This is the person on campus who will set the tone for the school's attitude toward your child, and will choose your child's teachers.

- Keep a list of goals and objectives (or the equivalent) to keep the school accountable for your child's progress or lack of progress.

- Have an evaluation system in place that accurately keeps track of your child's academic progress; this must be a system that is in addition to the teachers' grades.

- Become familiar with evaluation.

- Come up with a data collection system that tracks your child's social behavior in a variety of social settings. Have the speech therapist work on those identified social weaknesses that have been targeted.

- Be cautious of the tendency toward 'appeal to authority.' Just because someone has a doctorate, it does not follow that they are informed on your child's disability, or that they will work well with your child.

- Trust your instincts. When you are given information that does not sound correct, do some further research.

- When you find a professional you are comfortable with and you trust, continue to contact that person as often as possible.

- Monitor your child's school year. Remind the school of the obligations they have agreed to fulfill (e.g., evaluations, grades).

- Have a plan in place of what you think needs to happen if your child does not make the expected progress.

- Watch for reading comprehension scores. Students can often decode well, but they may have difficulty comprehending what they are reading. This will not necessarily be detected in the overall reading evaluation score. You must look at the evaluation subtest scores, which list comprehension, and look for any problems there.

- Do not allow yourself to be rushed through IEP meetings.

- Come to your IEP meetings with your agenda written down. Let the school staff address their own concerns first. If some issues are brought up that are listed on your agenda, check them off as they are discussed. When the agenda prepared by the school is finished, then address the remaining items on your list.

- Push staff to become informed on your child's disability through conferences, literature, videotapes, and consultants.

- Do not expect campus staff to be knowledgeable on the laws that govern your child's education – often they have not received training in this area.

Chapter Six

Becoming Resourceful

Accepting the disability

When Ryan was first diagnosed, we did not know anyone in our age group who had a child with a disability. Matt had two cousins with Down's Syndrome, but neither of us had much contact with them. DeAnn had grown up with a brother who had been diagnosed with learning disabilities, and when she was a child, her next-door neighbor had a daughter, Tara, with mental retardation and so the concept of disabilities and their ramifications did not escape either of us.

DeAnn remembers her mother spending hours working with her brother on homework, making sure it was completed and making sure it was handed in, and making the ninety-minute round trip to Omaha each week to get her brother to his occupational therapy sessions. In the early 1960s, many teachers did not accept the concept of learning disabilities – they thought DeAnn's brother was just lazy. Her mother often went to the school to speak with one teacher or another about how they treated him. She was also extremely active with the Parent Teacher Association (PTA), which allowed her to keep in close contact with the teachers. The school superintendent and DeAnn's parents were very good friends; they made use of his position on several occasions. Each school year, DeAnn's mother was allowed to choose her son's teachers. DeAnn's parents became involved with parenting classes. DeAnn's mother also found a counselor for her brother, so for several years DeAnn, both her brothers, and her mother went to Omaha on Saturday mornings. As involved and informed as DeAnn's mother was, she did not realize until years later the extent of the insensitivity of his teachers.

Both DeAnn's brother and Tara attended the local school. The elementary school, junior high school, and high school had a combined total of some 1000 students. DeAnn can remember the horrible teasing and taunting that her brother and her neighbor had to endure from the other students. She also remembers how cruel the teachers were to several students with disabilities. DeAnn's parents and Tara's parents were aware of the problems with teachers, and fortunately when DeAnn's brother started junior high school, the teachers became more accepting of him. This was at about the time when DeAnn's father was a member of the local school board. Though the abuse from the teachers ceased, the teasing from the other students went on.

When Ryan was initially diagnosed, we trusted that the education system would do the best possible for Ryan. The laws had changed since DeAnn's brother had been in school, and now teachers were trained in how to work with children like Ryan – or so we thought. It did not take long to realize that while there were laws that guaranteed that Ryan was to receive a Free Appropriate Public Education, it was very unlikely that Ryan's educational needs would be met unless we both educated ourselves on what he needed. The challenge was that in addition to having to learn about Ryan's disability and how to address his needs at home, we also had to learn educational law and what the teachers/therapists should be doing with him. As parents in our first encounter with the public school system, it was difficult to locate the resources we needed to determine what Ryan needed and how to get the school district to provide these services.

With the help of counseling, we were able to accept that Ryan had a disability. DeAnn began talking to other parents of children with autism/PDD, and she became involved in a local support group. She found that she could talk to other parents and learn about discipline techniques, books to read, professionals to use, and professionals to avoid. She learned about the politics of the local school system, and how other parents had gone about getting support for their child. The benefit of talking with other parents was that she learned from others who were in the trenches. They did not offer advice that had not worked. They were not like the professionals, who went home to their families and had a break from it all – they were people who lived with their children and their disability for twenty-four hours, seven days a week.

Working with agencies

Talking to other parents gave us access to the various types of agencies that offered community support for children with PDD. There is a vast array of these. DeAnn discovered, however, that the person who answered the telephone did not always know about the different types of funding, or who to talk to. Trying to find out what services were offered without prior knowledge of the agency was an exercise in futility. Other parents helped to expedite the process by telling us beforehand the specific agency, the name of the funding, and the name of the person with whom to talk. Other parents were also knowledgeable about what types of interventions and support were funded, and how to fill out the paperwork for the intervention. Another benefit of talking to parents about each agency was the benefit of comparing notes on who had been told what; it reduced the likelihood of accepting misinformation from the staff at the agency.

Anyone who has dealings with bureaucracies will discover that the employees are overworked and underpaid. The caseload for most of these employees is mind-boggling. Many employees are also undertrained, which leads to them conveying misinformation. Additionally, although many agencies refer to their employees as the family's advocates, in reality they are often the gatekeepers. An informed parent can learn to identify the gatekeepers and accelerate the process of getting services in the community for their child. We learned to keep copies of all paperwork when dealing with an agency. Keeping a journal of what had been discussed when and with whom saved us a great deal of time and frustration. It is the parents, not a case manager, who have the knowledge of what their child needs, and so we informed the case manager of what Ryan needed, and not the reverse, as we have seen many parents allow. We discovered that many of the techniques we had learned from working with the public school system could be effectively applied to the community agencies.

It is important to note that funding outside the school system can augment the services being received in school. The school is responsible for providing what is educationally necessary. Here again we found helpful information from other parents on what supports and interventions had worked for their child. They also described what interventions were not effective and which professionals to avoid.

Auditory retraining was one such area where parent information led us to the intervention, the funding, and the professional. We talked with many families before making the decision to attempt it. Ryan had over-sensitive hearing — dogs, crying children, and train whistles were excruciatingly painful for him. We were hesitant to proceed with the auditory retraining until we checked to make sure there were no harmful side effects. We did not discover any through our research. At the time, insurance did not cover the cost of the training. We found state funding as a result of talking to other parents. We also found the professional who could administer it. All three of us noticed an immediate difference in Ryan's hearing sensitivity.

Attendant care was another service we found through funding. We had been fortunate when we lived in the Dallas/Fort Worth area, where we had grandparents, aunts, uncles, and cousins. In West Texas we were on our own, and as we were hesitant to leave Ryan with someone we did not know very well, it was very difficult for us to find time for ourselves. One program we found offered respite that consisted of taking the child to a facility where there were other children with autism. We had worked very hard to provide Ryan with an opportunity to be with his typical peers, so this type of program went against our philosophy of Inclusion. For two years we had no opportunity to go out without Ryan. Finally, DeAnn found a program that provided an attendant of our choice, and the attendant watched Ryan at our home. One year we chose a person who was completing her occupational therapy internship, another year a neighbor who was completing her master's degree in education. We also managed, along the way, to hire the speech therapist and one of Ryan's elementary school teachers. The program finally allowed the attendant to take Ryan out into the community to work on his social skills.

Finding therapies

Speech therapy was another service we managed to procure outside the school system. It took several phone calls to find a speech therapist who was willing to focus on language pragmatics which is the functional and practical use of social language. Ryan functions so well with his language skills that professionals sometimes miss that he has trouble in the social arena. The added intervention has enabled Ryan to build on the skills he learned from the speech therapist at school.

We have also managed to obtain occupational therapy outside the school setting. The district does provide occupational therapy, but only to the extent that is documented as educationally necessary. The therapist and DeAnn felt that Ryan needed additional therapy. The therapist also used pet therapy in her sessions, and her combination of pet therapy, sensory integration, and occupational therapy has been effective for Ryan. The pet therapy helped not only with Ryan's tactile defensiveness but also with his fear of animals. Until she had worked with him, Ryan disliked dogs; we think this was because their barking hurt his ears. The therapist's puppy, Bridgett, was the first dog Ryan had ever tolerated. He then began interacting with her other dogs, particularly one called Peaches. After the dogs, Ryan began to enjoy petting cats. One day a brown-and-gray tabby kitten showed up on our doorstep. DeAnn felt sorry for it and made the mistake of feeding it. It stayed. Ryan named it 'Summer Lightning.' We are now the proud owners of a cat (or the cat owns us – we aren't sure). Summer Lightning is very patient with Ryan, up to a point. Every once in a while Ryan will complain that the cat has scratched him. When we ask Ryan what he did, we rarely get an answer.

After-school therapies and activities have included occupational therapy, speech therapy, reading programs, the Fun Club, swimming, soccer, and tae kwon do. As often as possible we have tried to involve Ryan's typical peers, so Ryan could be working on social skills in the community.

Of all the therapies, hippotherapy/equine therapy (horse riding therapy) has been our favorite. When Ryan turned thirteen, he grew very tall very quickly. Despite sensory integration and occupational therapy, it seemed as though he lost some of his motor coordination skills. As it turned out, this is typical of growing adolescents. One day, when we were out of town at a friend's house, Ryan was kneeling on a skateboard. The skateboard stopped suddenly in a crack in the sidewalk, Ryan fell face forward, and he knocked out his two front teeth. His reflexes did not tell him to put his hands in front to catch himself. We were fortunate to find a dentist who put the teeth back within the hour. Afterward, DeAnn approached the occupational therapist about hippotherapy, as she had just read an article about someone who had recently started a program in our area.

When Ryan first started, it was surprising that he had enough balance to stay on the horse. Soon Ryan began to perform various exercises on the horse, such as standing still, riding backwards, and so on. We were amazed at the progress Ryan made with his gross motor skills within a few weeks – even his handwriting improved. After a year of hippotherapy, which involves a therapist such as an occupational therapist or speech therapist, Ryan was switched to equine therapy, which does not require the participation of the therapist. Ryan began to learn to ride. Currently Ryan is riding on an English saddle and learning how to jump. When Ryan first started riding, the therapist said that she would probably put Ryan on her horse, John. She explained that John was a peculiar horse in that some days he did not want to be touched or petted. After two years, John is always excited to see Ryan, and now he does enjoy Ryan petting him.

At first, the program was conducted on a ranch, secluded from other riders. Eventually, it moved to a regular stable. To kick off the program moving to the stables, the owners had a horse show. Ryan and the other children were invited to participate. Because of Ryan's ability to ride, he was allowed to compete in some of the same activities as the typical riders. One such event was called Ride a Buck. Ryan won first place because he rode bareback and could keep a dollar under his leg. Ryan and John won a halter as their prize.

Ryan now makes money by going to the stables and working. There are usually other kids at the stables working with their horses, and Ryan has the opportunity to interact with the others in a very typical fashion. He also has training in a variety of naturally occurring occupational therapy skills. While feeding the horses, he has to get the bales of hay, load them in the wheelbarrow, roll it over to the horse, use wire cutters to cut the baling wire, and so on. At the same time, he is learning pre-vocational skills and the responsibility of taking care of the horses.

Disciplining

In addition to locating supports and services in the community, it became clear early on that we would have to teach Ryan skills if he was to be successful in the community. From the beginning, professionals would state that Ryan was not like any other child with autism with whom they had worked before. We knew that as Ryan's parents we would have to research interventions and sometimes just figure out on our own what it was that Ryan needed. A type of discipline method was one such intervention that we had to develop.

We learned early on that novel situations were very difficult for Ryan. Sometimes he would withdraw and shut down; at other times he would go into what we now know as sensory overload and have a temper tantrum. We started to explain to Ryan ahead of time what to expect in unique situations. This required us to think through the upcoming event and anticipate what might happen. Then one of us would outline to Ryan what would probably happen and what behavior was expected from him, and we would give him some options. Once we were in the situation, we would watch Ryan carefully, sometimes prompting him along the way. At times we would have to leave early if Ryan was having a difficult time. If we waited too long, we would leave with an out-of-control child, kicking and screaming. Others were quick to pass judgment on our parenting. We were often told that we were spoiling Ryan by not punishing him. At other times we were accused of being overprotective. But we knew that even though we did not always know why Ryan responded the way he did, spanking and/or forcing him to stay in the environment was not the answer.

Transitions were another area that was very difficult for Ryan. Again, one of us would try to anticipate and forewarn Ryan of the upcoming change. For instance, when we were getting ready to leave, we would give ten-minute warnings and then five-minute warnings. This has always been helpful for Ryan. When going into a new environment, we again try to anticipate and talk to Ryan beforehand. We try to eliminate or reduce the impact of any novel situation as much as possible.

We also discovered that Ryan did not respond well to physical punishment. Spanking him only escalated the situation. Often he would simply hit back, which seemed to defeat the whole purpose of punishment. He never accepted that adults could hit, but he should not. We both came from families that used spanking as a discipline – we were at a loss when it came to other methods of disciplining. As a family, we came up with a 'no hit' rule. No one in the household was allowed to hit another individual. Then we developed a contract system, with several rules that were numbered. When Ryan broke a rule, he had to complete the contract. As Ryan had a difficult time with handwriting, the contract required very little writing. He had to write down the number of the rule he had broken, circle the name of the emotion he thought he and his parents would feel as a result, and list his offense and what he would do differently. Then one of us would talk with him about the contract. Sometimes Ryan would escalate the situation and incur several contracts. The first contract had no consequence other than the contract itself. All other subsequent contracts had consequences, such as the loss of a privilege like playing on his Nintendo. Ryan could work off his consequences by performing a chore that would help the family, such as folding the clean laundry or doing the evening dishes. The contract system became a very effective intervention. It provided us with a method of talking to Ryan about his actions and allowed us to discuss 'theory of mind' (other people's perspective) and options for behavior in the future. For Ryan, it was routine and consistent, and it used both his auditory and his visual modes of learning. For us, it was not punishment, it was discipline.

We also found that for Ryan it was helpful to label behavior. Instead of chastising Ryan for interrupting (which never seemed to make an impact), we would say, 'That's interrupting.' If he talked back, we would say, 'That's talking back.' This helped Ryan to identify the behavior and enabled him to adjust his interactions accordingly. We would also explain to him his choices in changing his behavior. For example, when he interrupted us, we would label the behavior and then prompt him as to when he could talk in order to help him to identify appropriate times to join in the conversation. We found that the most important aspect of whatever discipline method we chose was to be consistent.

Teaching social skills

We also discovered that we had to teach Ryan sarcasm and teasing. It took almost two years of practicing for Ryan to learn to identify sarcasm in other people. How to respond to teasing and how to tease also took a great deal of time and effort, but he did learn. Idioms, double meanings, facial expressions, prosody, jokes, and body language are all areas we have had to teach him explicitly. We did this by discussing these skills with him and having him identify what he thought the other person was conveying. We found that talking these through was the best way for Ryan to learn. Recently Ryan indignantly told DeAnn that she had given him a 'snotty look.' This was a breakthrough for us – it showed that Ryan was learning to watch for facial expressions.

Some years ago Ryan came home with a joke he had heard at school. He laughed as he conveyed the story line to us. We looked at each other when he had delivered the punch line. We were shocked – it was a very dirty joke. Based on his laughter, one would have assumed that he understood the joke. When we asked him what was funny about the joke, he said he did not know. Together, we explained the joke to him. Ryan laughed and laughed when he understood the joke. Suddenly he stood up and said, 'I have to call Dora and tell her the joke.' Dora was one of his elementary school teachers and his surrogate grandmother. We had to explain genres of jokes and that some were not appropriate, depending on the audience.

We used Ryan's need for routine to help him to establish basic hygiene regimes. The routine for the morning is: putting on deodorant, getting dressed, washing your face, combing your hair, eating breakfast, and then brushing your teeth. Nighttime involves bathing, getting a snack, brushing your teeth, and going to bed. Ryan is very dependable in his daily hygiene, and he is very conscientious about looking well groomed.

Dressing was only an issue as far as textures of clothes were concerned. We had to be extremely careful with regard to fabric and stitching. Ryan could not abide pockets, decals, or decorative stitching on his shirts. He also had a difficult time with tying shoelaces, so for years we bought him shoes with Velcro fasteners while the occupational therapist worked on teaching Ryan how to tie laces. It was a disappointment when he outgrew shoes made with

Velcro, but eventually he did learn to tie his shoelaces. Because of his tactile defensiveness, Ryan prefers wearing shorts, and for years he protested whenever the weather required that he wear blue jeans. He also has the sleeves of long-sleeved shirts always pushed up above his elbows. We learned a long time ago to take him shopping and have him decide whether the garment passed the texture and color test. Ryan would only wear blue, if we allowed it. We watch as other boys his age leave school, and we take note of what they are wearing, so that we can guide Ryan's decisions on what clothes to purchase. We also check Ryan before he heads out the door, to double-check how he is dressed. Fortunately, he has started checking in the mirror, so only seldom do we ever have to say anything to him.

Telephone skills were an area that we soon learned we had to develop in Ryan. We had to plot out scripts on what he would say to the person he called. When he spoke to his grandparents, we stood close by to help limit him talking about his preservative interests. We had to teach him how to listen to the speaker and respond to questions. Ryan had to be taught to say 'hello' and 'good-bye.' We also had to teach him not to just pick up the phone when it rang and ask, 'Who is this?' Ryan has made tremendous progress in telephone skills. Though we stay close by in case he gets stuck, we do not have to monitor the conversations as closely.

Ryan acquiring appropriate table manners was a full-time endeavor that lasted several years. Because of his deficient fine motor skills, he has a difficult time holding and using utensils. He also had a difficult time learning how to chew. Eating with his mouth closed and not smacking were the most difficult table-manner skills for him to obtain. We usually have our family meal during the evening and on weekends during breakfast. Both of us work with Ryan, reminding him of table manners. When we eat out, we have Ryan read the menu and order for himself. He is responsible for ordering food the way he wants it (e.g., no cheese on his food). He has to negotiate with the serving staff if the food is prepared incorrectly. At age sixteen, Ryan's table manners are better than those of many of his typical peers.

Ryan's sense of etiquette out in the community is a skill we have had to develop. He is expected to be courteous and to say 'please' and 'thank you.' He also now opens doors for women and elderly people. DeAnn has had many women tell her, 'Good going, Mom.'

The grocery store is another area where we have worked on building social skills. In the beginning, Ryan was reluctant to go to the store. He would become angry and kick other customer's carts. DeAnn made an agreement: if Ryan came shopping with her, then he could be sure to get the items he wanted to eat for the week. Now Ryan goes to the store with DeAnn almost every week. He is now responsible for finding the items that he wants. This forces him to locate items on the store shelf, which, in turn, helps him with visual discrimination. Ryan is proficient enough in the store that DeAnn can now send him in by himself for a few items. He even gets the correct change back.

Sports were also an arena that required our creative input. Sports are an effective means of teaching social skills with typical peers. We tried soccer through a program that was non-competitive. Even so, soccer required too much teamwork for Ryan. We switched to tae kwon do. Before he started, we talked to the instructor about Ryan's problems. She was wonderful in working with Ryan. Tae kwon do helped Ryan to establish control, concentration, and gross motor skills. It also allowed him to interact with his peers in a very structured environment. Swimming also helped Ryan, by developing his coordination and his gross motor skills. Again, we always spoke to the instructors to educate them about Ryan. One of us stayed to monitor how well Ryan and the instructor were doing in the activity. We made sure before Ryan took any Physical Education (PE) class that the personality of the coach was one that would be accepting of Ryan's issues. DeAnn talked to each coach ahead of time and made sure they knew about Asperger Syndrome. So far, Ryan has enjoyed all PE Classes.

We found that many typical activities helped Ryan with coordination and social interaction. Board games and card games helped with reciprocity, taking turns, and learning how to win or lose. Chess turned out to be a wonderful activity for him to develop cognitive skills, in addition to being another avenue for interaction. We moved close to a park and we made sure we lived close to a swimming pool, so he would have access to his typical peers. Our park had a tree where Matt taught Ryan how to climb – a very typical skill for any child, but for Ryan it was another way of sneaking in an intervention we knew he needed.

Developing daily living skills

Now that Ryan is a growing adolescent, he is always hungry. One of DeAnn's hobbies is to cook, so Ryan has been exposed to the kitchen for several years. To teach him how to prepare his own food has not been difficult. DeAnn makes sure that he has snacks that he can prepare himself. He can put them into the oven, microwave them, or heat them on the stove. Gradually we are working him toward preparing a meal one night a week. We have noticed that in preparing his own snacks, Ryan is experimenting with different types of food textures and different combinations, especially when he is making his dessert. He enjoys ice cream with different types of cookies and chocolate syrups. As a result, he is getting more courageous with trying other types of food.

Ryan has chores that he is expected to perform. One is unloading the dishwasher; another is setting the table. We noticed that while Ryan was setting the table, he would get one plate and put it on the table, then take another plate and set it on the table. Just putting the plates on the table took three trips. He did the same with place mats, each piece of silverware, and the glasses. We have had to work with Ryan, teaching him to consolidate trips. It did not occur to him to reduce his workload. We had to turn it into a game of seeing how few trips back and forth he needs to set the table.

Paying a child to clean the house was something we swore we would never do. Now we joke and say, 'We got past that.' It was clear that Ryan would work for money when nothing else would motivate him to clean, and we decided that it was important that Ryan learns these skills and if money were the motivator in the beginning we would put our principles aside. He is now paid to sort laundry, vacuum, dust, unload the dishwasher, and so on. We will not, however, pay him to pick up his own room.

Living with the idiosyncrasies of Asperger Syndrome

Getting Ryan out of his self-imposed routines was one of our first challenges. When he was small, he would become very upset if we drove home a different way. We discovered that by telling him in advance that we were taking a different route home helped. We realized that we could not allow Ryan to dictate the way we came home, so we intentionally varied our route. Ryan's objections diminished.

Early on, Ryan had a tendency to prefer to stay at home. He had limited interest in getting out into the community. While we were in graduate school, it was easy for us to let a whole weekend go by without leaving the apartment, but it was not a healthy habit for Ryan. DeAnn came up with a rule that Ryan had to go out at least once a day. They would go to Dairy Queen, the park, McDonalds – anywhere where he could interact with other children. Whenever he was with other children, Ryan was never left unsupervised. At least one of us was always present in case there was some type of social crisis. DeAnn studied while Ryan played. The habit of getting out once a day is now an established part of Ryan's routine, and he himself insists that he gets out into the community each day.

Because of DeAnn's job, she travels quite a bit. In the beginning it was very difficult for Ryan when his mom was away. We learned, however, that it was good for Ryan to experience a change in routine. It helped father and son to develop a closer relationship. We also travel as a family whenever possible. Again, this was very difficult for Ryan at first, but it was necessary. The traveling has helped break up Ryan's routine, and it has given him the benefit of seeing a variety of people and places.

Organizing Ryan's environment has been another skill-building area. Both at home and at school we have had to help Ryan to learn to structure his environment. He has a difficult time locating items – he just cannot seem to find them, even if they are right in front of him. The solution is to make sure that every item has its place. This limits the frustration of Ryan not being able to locate something and one of us having to look for it.

Some aspects of Ryan's Asperger Syndrome have been extremely frustrating for us. For a short time Ryan would talk to himself. At first we were concerned about this behavior, until we realized that Ryan was talking through situations he had encountered. He was very careful that his windows were closed and that no one was visiting when he talked to himself. After a couple of years, the behavior disappeared. Another problematic behavior was that for six months Ryan got up every night and came to our room to tell us that there was an angry lady at the foot of his bed. No amount of discussion or reassurance would convince him there was no angry lady in his room. We were exhausted by the interruptions to our sleep. Some nights we would have him sleep on a pallet in our room, just so we could get a full night's sleep. Finally, the angry lady left, and Ryan stopped waking us up.

Another behavior stemming from Asperger Syndrome that caused trouble was that Ryan could not look at butter without throwing up. This behavior first started when he was five years old. We were eating breakfast at a local restaurant, and the waiter had just brought the butter for our croissants. All of a sudden, Ryan started gagging and vomiting and had to be rushed out the door. We thought that Ryan had a stomach bug. A few days later, he again unexpectedly started gagging and vomiting. Before long we realized that Ryan was becoming ill any time he looked at butter. This made absolutely no sense to us until we learned about sensory dysfunction. For years, we had to cover or hide the butter whenever we ate. It was only after a couple of years of sensory integration that Ryan was able overcome his reaction to the sight of butter.

Giggling is a behavior that caused great difficulty until recently. For Ryan it is a release of energy, a type of self-stimulation. It was a problem when he would giggle in school, but after a few years he has managed to control his giggling when in public. He still has a need to giggle at home, but it has greatly diminished over the years.

Ryan's preservative topics have added an interesting twist to our lives. He would talk about these topics nonstop. We finally had to start putting a time limit on how long and how often he could talk about these topics. We also had to instruct him as to when and where it was appropriate to talk about these interests. Ryan's favorite has always been blue oscillating fans. However, we have had other themes that move in and out of our lives. We have had interests in the solar system, the weather (particularly lightning), the Three Stooges, and currently early 1980s music. As it is very difficult to buy presents for Ryan, it is a relief when he establishes a new interest. Both of us, as well as DeAnn's side of the family, try to buy items that relate to his new interest.

Some of these preservations have had unexpected positive outcomes. One example is the 1980s music. Ryan was determined that he would learn how to dance to this music, but when he was shown a few steps, it was upsetting to see how badly he kept to the rhythm of the beat. Having tried several times to teach Ryan how to dance on beat, to no avail, DeAnn finally decided that rather than being discouraged, Ryan needed to have fun with the music. Several months later we were surprised to see how well Ryan had learned to keep beat to the music.

We have learned to be careful about attributing all behaviors to Asperger Syndrome. Ryan is a very normal teenager, and what might seem odd behavior to us as adults, such as angry outbursts, is actually very typical. We were recently reminded that we sometimes falsely attribute certain behavior to Asperger Syndrome. We were describing to one of Ryan's teachers how he used to sleep in his closet when he was five. We lived in an older house at the time, and Matt had built shelves in Ryan's closet for his toys. One day, Ryan cleared off the lower shelf, put his pillow and blanket on it, and climbed in to sleep there. He used it as his bed for months. We commented to Ryan's teacher that this behavior must have been a result of his sensory overload. Later that day we asked Ryan if he remembered sleeping in his closet, and he answered that he did. When we asked him about our sensory overload theory, he informed us that we were wrong: he wasn't doing it because of sensory overload – he was imitating one of Matt's brothers, who lived in an apartment at the time. He looked up to this uncle, so he was pretending that he was his uncle and lived in an apartment. So much for our theory.

We have had several parents ask us how old Ryan was when we told him that he had Asperger Syndrome. When he was seven, he asked DeAnn if he had autism, and she told him that he did. He knew another boy his age with autism, and he wanted to know why he could talk when the other boy could not. DeAnn explained to Ryan that he had a different form of autism, and we began to talk to Ryan about his disability, and that although it made some things very difficult for him, such as social interaction, it had also given him some gifts, such as a great memory. As much as possible, we have tried to help him come to terms with the disorder. For a short time Ryan felt that people should accept his odd behavior because he had autism, so we explained that he always had a choice when it came to his behavior, but with some behaviors the world would think he was odd, and people would shun him. When we saw an unusual behavior, we would ask him, 'Who's in charge, you or the autism?' While we want him to accept his disability, we also want him to be aware of its impact on other people around him. To date, Ryan says that he is proud he has Asperger Syndrome.

Empathy

Around Christmas John, the horse that Ryan rode for therapy, became very ill. At first his owner thought that he had colic, but it was discovered that he had a blockage that had to be surgically removed. John was twenty-one, and so the vet was very pessimistic that he would survive the surgery. Although he did survive, John then developed peritonitis, and for several weeks, he was literally dying. The vet had even given up all hope of his survival and had stopped providing medical care. John's owner went to visit him on New Year's Eve. Because John was too ill to get up and stand, she left with the expectation that John would have to be put down the next day. We were out of town, but we kept in contact with John's owner during this time. On New Year's Day, when the vet arrived at the clinic, he was shocked to discover John standing and pawing at the gate and decided to begin medical treatment again, and John came home. Ryan talked with John's owner about walking John on a daily basis to help build up his muscle tone and announced to her: 'John made me the man I am today.' Ryan has been very committed to John's full recovery, and he refers to himself as John's rehab therapist. John has not been the most cooperative of patients. He has tried to run off while Ryan was putting on his halter, he has refused to walk, and he would rear up a little to intimidate Ryan. John's handler has shown Ryan what to do in these situations – he has had to learn to watch John's body language and attempt to anticipate his actions. He has also had to learn how to discipline John. When we watch Ryan with John, we are filled with pride that he has managed to develop such empathy and caring for an animal. This is a big step for Ryan – something he would not have been capable of doing a very short time ago.

The following June, John's owner called to invite us out to the stables. For the first time since his illness at Christmas, John was going to be released in the big pen without a lead. We brought our video camera to document the event, and together the owner and Ryan led John to the big pen while a small group of us stood outside, watching. After a few private words they stroked John and released him from the lead. It took a couple of seconds for John to realize that he was not on the lead, then he kicked up his heels and galloped off, stopped at the end of the fence, turned around, neighed, and galloped at full speed to the opposite corner. We all talked with Ryan about how walking John all those months he had made this day possible. This event allowed Ryan to see the fruits of his labors. After a few minutes of prancing and galloping, the owner had John follow her without a lead. We were told that a horse that knows someone very well and is comfortable with him/her will follow that person without a lead. To date, John had only done this with his owner. He had always been partial to her, to the exclusion of anyone else, if she was present. Ryan was instructed to try. We held our breath. Ryan walked, and John followed. Ryan beamed. Ryan and John had made that all-important social connection.

What we learned

We learned to become extremely resourceful on many levels, and we came to appreciate the value of talking with other parents about school districts, interventions, and legal strategies. As we communicated with others, we became more comfortable sharing stories and we discovered that we were not alone in our struggles – others were having some of the same difficulties. The support did not have to come from a support group – it could come from a friend.

We had to learn to find interventions outside the school system, which is responsible only for what is educationally appropriate. Ryan needed more, and so we found speech therapists, occupational therapists, and an equine therapist. To help Ryan further with communication skills, we enrolled him in sports and had him work with horses; these helped him to generalize the skills he had learned from therapy and school. To help him develop a sense of responsibility, we had him work at the stables, take care of a cat, and learn to do household chores. In as many ways as we could think of, we tried to provide Ryan with opportunities to interact and learn from his environment.

Since we lived so far from our families, we had to find people who would take an interest in Ryan. Fortunately, we found two surrogate grandmothers and others who were willing to spend time with Ryan. A couple of Ryan's teachers and one of his therapists spent time with him each week, and the horse owners helped Ryan to learn to work with their horses. All these people helped to expose Ryan to experiences and situations that helped to build on what we were already teaching him.

Together, we learned to trust our instincts in developing interventions for Ryan. Because we could find no information about Ryan's disorder, we had to follow our intuition in learning to meet his needs. We had to watch and interpret as best we could what his behavior was telling us. At times it was difficult to distinguish between Ryan's sensory issues and when he needed discipline. Sometimes we could figure out why he was responding a particular way; at other times we were not sure. We were both comfortable enough with our instincts to push the school district into providing specific supports. We could tell by the way Ryan responded to various interventions whether we were on the right track or not. Fortunately, in most cases we were correct. When information started to be published on Asperger Syndrome, we were surprised to find that we had been right in what we had pushed so hard for the educators and other professionals to do for Ryan.

PDD-NOS and autism did not describe Ryan. Because until recently Asperger Syndrome was not known in the United States, we had to be resourceful in working with him. We have had to walk a fine line between respecting Ryan's individuality and teaching him how to fit into society. Our successes with Ryan so far have helped us to develop self-confidence in the decisions we make for him. We have learned to be flexible, anticipating as much as possible what Ryan will need next. When we see that we need to make a major change in what we are doing, we sit down, talk about our options, and develop a plan. We are hopeful that our flexibility and resourcefulness will continue to help us to provide the love and support that Ryan needs to develop into a successful young man.

What you can do

- Find emotional support through a friend or family member.

- Insist on teacher training for your child's disability issues. In the United States the training can be required through the Individuals with Disability Education Act (IDEA).

- Talk to other parents about schools, interventions, and agencies.

- Talk to parents of older children with a similar disability. They have already experienced some similar issues (e.g., ages and stages), and they can help you anticipate upcoming stages of development.

- Do not expect the receptionist at an agency to know who it is that you need to talk to about particular services.

- Do not expect case managers or service coordinators to be effective advocates for your child; they are usually untrained in specific disability issues, and they carry outrageously big caseloads.

- Parents are the one constant in their child's life; professionals will come and go.

- Keep copies of all agency paperwork.

- Keep a journal listing everyone you talk to; the person's name and the date and time of day of the conversation, and write a brief overview of what was discussed.

- Look for services outside the school system to augment those the school provides.

- Look for opportunities in the community for your child to interact with typical children – sports, community groups, church groups, and so on.
- Look for sports that your child can learn to be successful at and in which the child can participate with other children.
- When out in the community, watch for opportunities for teaching.
- Teach your child manners.
- Locate regular respite for you and your spouse.
- Find a discipline method that teaches the behavior you want.
- Label your child's behavior (e.g., 'that's talking back,' 'that's interrupting').
- Be consistent with discipline.
- Research various types of interventions and therapies.
- Interview and talk with the therapist before having your child participate in the therapy.
- Consider animals and pets to encourage interaction and nonverbal learning skills.

Assessing a speech therapist: what to look for

- Talk to the therapist before taking your child there.
- Ask if the therapist is trained in working with language pragmatics.

- Speech therapists make a distinction between speech and language; be clear which you are interested in:
  - *Speech* is the sounds that come from our mouths and form words;
  - *Language* consists of *receptive language* and *expressive language:*
    - *Receptive language* is the comprehension of speech, prosody, body language, gestures, facial expressions, and so on.
    - *Expressive language* is the means by which a person communicates while speaking.
- Ask if they are familiar with your child's disability.
- Ask how they will work with your child.
- Show the speech therapist your child's Individual Education Plan.
- Have the speech therapist assess your child.
- Sit down with the speech therapist and discuss what you want him/her to work on.
- Ask if they are willing to work with your child and another child together. Some children who receive speech therapy do not have social difficulties and can be excellent speech buddies.
- Make sure this is someone both you and your child are comfortable with.

Chapter Seven

From Parents
to Parent/Professionals

Parents

After Ryan was diagnosed with Pervasive Developmental Disorder Not Otherwise Specified (PDD-NOS), we discovered that the professionals working with Ryan had limited knowledge about PDD-NOS and how to work with someone who had the disorder, and we began the difficult process of becoming informed about the PDD spectrum in order to be able to persuade the professionals to work more effectively with Ryan. This process involved becoming informed about the PDD spectrum, about the laws governing special education, and about appropriate interventions to meet Ryan's specific needs. Obtaining the appropriate services and supports for Ryan became a time-consuming endeavor. As beginning parents in the Individual Education Plan (IEP) process, we depended on the educators to help guide the procedures for developing an appropriate education plan for Ryan. Not only are very few parents trained in the education process, they also tend to be intimidated and overwhelmed at the meetings. We were both surprised to learn when we took graduate-level courses in special education for teachers and diagnosticians that special education law received little if any discussion in the class on the IEP process. Additionally, we found that school counselors are made responsible for IEP paperwork even though they have received no formal education on the Individuals with Disabilities Education Act (IDEA), and that many professionals in the education field have very limited knowledge of the IEP process. We discovered that families and professionals are all struggling with a lack of information on how to develop and write up an appropriate education plan. As our knowledge and self-confidence grew, we began to share our experiences and our knowledge with other families and professionals through workshops and presentations and by writing articles.

Becoming informed

When we attended our first IEP meeting, we entered a room full of people already sitting at a large round table, where two chairs had been left vacant for us. As we sat down, we felt surrounded. The counselor had attempted to prepare us for the meeting, but she had confessed that she herself knew very little about IEP meetings. We both just sat and listened and nodded our heads as the professionals went around the table, reading their reports. All Ryan's deficits they had found were listed, sometimes including new and upsetting information. We felt that this information should have been shared with us privately, instead of in front of a group of strangers. When the reports had been read, a plan that had already been drawn up was read aloud. Someone passed a paper around that everyone had to sign. Then it was over. The second IEP meeting, at the end of the year, was very similar to the first. We thought that the educators were trained in special education, and they would do what was best for Ryan; we trusted them, and we were naïve in doing so.

We requested the third meeting. After reading the federal and state laws, we had learned that we were supposed to be equal participants in the IEP development process. We had just discovered that the school was responsible for providing any educational evaluation and intervention that the IEP committee determined as appropriate, at no expense to us. Up to this time, the district had allowed us to pay for three evaluations and counseling services. Angry about the deception, we zealously researched the school's responsibilities when working with Ryan. The more we learned, the more hostile we became. We made the transition from naïve and trusting parents to 'warrior parents,' ready for battle.

When we talked with other parents in the district, we discovered that they, too, had had the same experience. It is not surprising that the parents who talked to other parents were angry. Soon we formed a small army of 'warrior parents.' As we talked and shared notes of meetings and conversations with the educators, we parents learned what services to request and whom to ask for these. We developed a network of resources to contact about education law, PDD, services, and appropriate interventions. We could also use one another to discuss tactics and strategies for the IEP meetings.

By the time we had the third IEP meeting, we were ready. We had all our research in the 'black bag.' The research had been highlighted and tabbed for speed and convenience. We had our tape recorder, with extra batteries and tapes, and our long list of questions and concerns. We had rehearsed with one another their possible arguments and positions. We were informed, and we had a chip on our shoulders.

Everyone was in the room waiting for us so they could begin. Our two vacant chairs were waiting for us. The educators had an odd look on their faces when we came in, with Matt carrying the bag. The moment we put the tape recorder in the middle of the table, their body posture and demeanor changed. With that one act, the battle lines had been drawn on both sides. Looking back, we are sure they had seen such transformations of parents before, and they knew the signs. They all probably wondered what had happened to us during the summer. Their placating attitude quickly changed to defensiveness, and we obliged them.

For the first time, we led the meeting. Instead of reports being read, we listed our concerns one by one. Each time someone brought up an objection, we countered it, backing it with our research. The IEP committee granted all our requests. We had proven our case, and we left feeling victorious. We debriefed after the meeting – we discussed who had said what, what we should have said, and what we would say next time. We also listened to the tape, critiquing our performance. We were developing skills that increased our level of participation in obtaining services and supports for Ryan's education.

From that IEP meeting onward, we researched different types of interventions, listed facts to back up our requests, rehearsed before each meeting, and debriefed afterwards. We also kept a journal listing everyone we talked to and giving the day and time as well as what was discussed. Any time we were denied a request, if we were not convinced with the rationale, we did more research, and came back with more proof. It became more and more difficult for the IEP committee simply to counter our requests with platitudes, as had been done early on.

Together, we began attending conferences on autism, Inclusion, and parenting. There, we would see other parents whom we knew, and the conferences became opportunities to meet and talk with other families. At the first few conferences on PDD that we attended, we realized that the district was not sending any professionals to the conference; after a period of time, we noticed that some professionals from our district were attending the same conferences.

By the end of Ryan's first-grade year, we had been actively involved in the IEP process for about a year. What we came to realize was that successfully obtaining an appropriate education for Ryan through our increased level of knowledge and our assertive attitude had come at a high price. We had alienated every professional on our committee, including Ryan's teacher. Each suggestion and recommendation we made was met with an air of defensiveness. We were begrudged every victory.

To try to remedy the situation, we found books on negotiation. *Getting to Yes* (Fisher, Ury and Patton, 1991) was the first book we read, and we practiced the strategies at the meetings. These strategies worked so well that we purchased the companion book, *Getting Past No* (Ury, 1993). Through these books and others like them we learned to remove our emotions from the meeting. We began operating at a more intellectual and professional level. We attempted to establish a comfortable relationship with Ryan's teachers, but they always seemed to be guarded around us. By the end of second grade, Ryan's special education teacher, whom we had known for two years, was extremely cool toward us. Just before we moved to West Texas, we heard that she had requested a transfer to and had been granted a general education classroom placement.

The transition to professional

When Ryan began school in West Texas, we brought the tape recorder and the black bag to the meetings with us. At the first IEP meeting, DeAnn refused to sign a form that stated that DeAnn had received and read the particular form. DeAnn pointed out to the IEP committee that she had not read it yet. The special education coordinator declared that every parent had to sign this form for the school's records, so DeAnn took her pen and crossed out that she had read the form. She wrote in that she had just been handed the form at the meeting, and she had not had an opportunity to read it. In the eyes of the IEP committee, DeAnn had made it known that she was an aggressive parent, and she knew it. She wanted to let everyone on the team know that she was not a passive parent. However, in the process she alienated two people to the point that we never got along with them after that day.

DeAnn started to connect up with other agencies in the area that informed her of various legal conferences. She began attending special education legal conferences as well as IEP meetings with other parents. As a result, she became very knowledgeable regarding federal and state guidelines. Matt began attending the training in Austin, and he was taking a master's level course on special education. At the IEP meetings, we had both developed some strategies that worked very well. DeAnn presented our recommendations and supported our position with research and legal facts. As DeAnn talked, Matt watched to see how the other committee members received the information. He observed their facial expressions and their body language, and he listened to what they said. When it was Matt who spoke, DeAnn did the same. We learned never to sit together. We arrived to the meetings early, and we chose our seats. Matt tried to sit next to the person whom we expected to be the most difficult person to work with – usually the special education coordinator – and DeAnn generally sat directly across from Matt. The principal picked up on this strategy. One day, laughing, he introduced us at an IEP meeting as 'the couple who never sit together.' We had become a very efficient and effective team.

It is important to note that as we became more informed and better skilled in the meetings, we were alienating the special education administration while we were developing friendships at the campus level, in particular with the principal. After the first couple of meetings we stopped bringing the tape recorder, and eventually we even stopped bringing our black bag. However, we always brought Ryan's most recent IEP, in addition to a list of our concerns. We did not encounter resistance to our recommendations from the campus staff. Before each IEP meeting, we met with the teacher, the principal, and the therapist to discuss IEP goals and objectives. We wanted to make sure that we were all pulling together. At these pre-IEP meetings we would ask the teacher whether they needed us to request anything for them. We learned that, as much as possible, we needed to advocate both for Ryan *and* for his teacher.

Parent/professionals

By 1994, DeAnn had also started graduate school. For one of her class projects she developed a workshop on the IEP process for parents. From her experience in attending IEP meetings with other families, she came to realize that parents were truly in the dark about the IEP process. Her workshop had several modules that took the parents through the process step by step.

After the semester was over, DeAnn took the manual to a parent organization in Amarillo and offered that if they would find a facility for her, print the handouts, and provide publicity, she would train the parents every other week for five weeks. They agreed, and DeAnn presented the workshop. After the workshops, DeAnn asked the parents for their recommendations to develop the presentation further.

Because the first workshop had taken several weeks to complete, DeAnn shortened the presentation to a one-day workshop. Based on the Amarillo parents' suggestions, she edited and performed it again, this time with Matt. The parents all said that they had enjoyed the workshop. A professor at the local university asked us to present for her class of diagnosticians, and we agreed, provided that parents could also participate. The professor agreed, and we made the presentation to student/professionals and parents. The questions that were asked demonstrated to all present that everyone is dealing with a lack of information. Parents and professionals left the workshop with a better understanding of the others' perspectives when in a meeting.

After our experience at the university, we requested that professionals attend the workshop alongside the parents. We realized the importance of parents and professionals learning the IEP process together. We realized that by learning together, parents and professionals would learn to understand one another better. The workshop involved a lot of filling in the blanks, so we began to request tables for the participants. We recognized that people generally want to sit next to someone they know well, so we developed a way to make the audience sit alternating parents and professionals at each table. We developed games and a mock IEP meeting to reinforce what we had taught during the day. The workshop grew to include evaluation, a mock IEP meeting, writing IEP goals and objectives, and finally with placement. Our evaluations showed that parents and professionals enjoyed the workshop and gained valuable information. The last time the workshop was presented, we had 120 participants.

We have traveled around Texas, providing this workshop. Whenever we can arrange for both of us to present it together, we do so. Experience has shown that generally fathers are not involved in the education process, leaving mothers to fend for themselves. Through our own experiences we have learned the importance of both parents participating in the IEP process. It is our hope that more fathers will get involved in the future.

IEP meetings

Shortly after we moved to West Texas, DeAnn began attending IEP meetings with other parents, which exposed her to a variety of issues and people who work in the school system. This helped her to develop skills for Ryan's IEP meetings. DeAnn's favorite meetings were those for families of children with autism and Asperger Syndrome. As a mother of a child with these issues, she knew the struggles parents faced in getting their child appropriate services. Because DeAnn, herself, had had to push for similar services, she had developed skills for obtaining them.

DeAnn attended an IEP meeting for a young man who had not been diagnosed with high functioning autism until he was sixteen. He had attended our social skills group for several months when his mother informed us that he was not talking in school. This information came as a complete surprise to us, since he talked in the group and had made great strides in interacting with the adults and other teens. When DeAnn appeared at the IEP meeting, the principal apologized and said that someone was running late, so the IEP meeting would have to be postponed for a little while. Within fifteen minutes, a special education coordinator appeared at the meeting. It was obvious that the IEP committee had called in last-minute reinforcements. Several items were discussed during the meeting, until finally the subject of this student not talking in school was addressed. The special education teacher and the speech therapist shared their opinion with the IEP committee on why they thought the student was not talking. They felt that he had stopped talking in order to gain 'attention.' 'Just look around this room and see how many people are sitting here, talking about this,' the teacher announced. 'He has obtained what he wants.' It was crystal clear that the adults wanted to put all the responsibility for the problem on the student, thus absolving the adults of their responsibility to continue to search for the cause of the problem.

After the meeting, the boy's mother continued to research her son's problem of not talking in school. After a few months, she took him to a psychiatrist, who diagnosed selective mutism. The student is now receiving interventions through a behavior management plan, and he has made great strides in talking with other students at school. DeAnn and the boy's mother have discussed several times how fortunate it is that neither of them accepted the 'attention-getting' theory.

Another IEP meeting involved an elementary school student who was not reading on grade level. The parents had requested a Brigance to establish his reading level. Because of the difficulties the family was having on one campus, they had requested a transfer to another campus, and somehow the results of the Brigance were lost in the transfer, and the parents decided to get an outside reading evaluation from a reading specialist. As they were preparing for the IEP meeting, the boy's father noticed on some documentation that the Individual Education Plan goals had been changed. The parents asked DeAnn to attend. Once again, the IEP committee was temporarily postponed because someone was running late. This time the district compliance officer appeared. The parents had several requests: (1) that the outside evaluation should be used to write goals and objectives; (2) that the outside evaluator should administer another evaluation in the spring to check on progress; (3) that the student should have tutoring in reading; (4) that the outside evaluator should be the tutor for the student. During the IEP meeting it became apparent that the committee did not want to accept the results of the outside evaluation but they wanted to do their own testing, nor were they willing to concede the parents' other requests. The compliance officer requested that a Brigance be administered. When she was informed that it had recently been administered and the results had been lost, she was obviously upset, but she still did not want to grant the parents' request. DeAnn asked for a recess and a private meeting with the parents and the compliance officer. At the meeting, the parents told the compliance officer about the altered IEP. In Texas, it is a felony to alter state records. At this point, the compliance officer knew that the district had a major problem. The IEP committee decided to grant the parents' requests, with the exception that a teacher would provide one-on-one tutoring instead of the outside evaluator.

One IEP committee meeting DeAnn attended illustrated quite clearly the difficulty school personnel have in seeing the social dysfunction of students with Asperger Syndrome. We are not the only ones who have a difficult time getting Ryan's school personnel to see his social difficulties and address them; other parents encounter the same struggle. This student was also in our social skills group, and her mother was very concerned that the school was not addressing her social needs in school. When DeAnn looked at the IEP, she agreed with the mother. DeAnn and a speech therapist in private practice attended the IEP meeting. The school commented on how well this child was doing academically – in fact, she was a straight A student. The speech therapist discussed the results of her evaluation, which clearly showed that the girl was struggling with pragmatic language. The school staff discussed how well she was interacting with the other students; citing several different examples, they shared how she was talking in the halls and carrying on conversations with teachers and her peers. From what the teachers were saying, it sounded as if this student had been 'cured.' After much discussion, the IEP committee agreed that as the student was correctly identified with Asperger Syndrome, she could not possibly be interacting this well. The school staff began going into detail about what they were seeing. The student was not consistently talking to her peers in the halls, or even initiating interactions such as 'hi.' When she was talking to other students and the teachers, she was talking exclusively about computers, which was her preservative topic. It was not until the IEP committee began analyzing and discussing the interactions that they saw this student's social disability. When they recognized what was happening, they were able to begin developing goals and objectives.

In each case listed, the school personnel were truly interested in helping each student. Each time, once the IEP committee understood what needed to be done, an appropriate education plan was developed. The obstacle in each instance was lack of information and training in the student's learning issues.

Graduate school taught us the perspective of the educators. Before, we had regarded the school staff as the 'other side,' but now we sat in class with many people who teach and work in the school system. We learned that the professionals are often at a loss as to what to do. No one gets into the education system expecting to make a lot of money. They are interested in teaching children. The professionals in the education system are overworked and underpaid. Classroom teachers often have little if any support from administration. With statewide accountability, many teachers have to worry about their students passing the state-mandated evaluation if they want a pay-raise or a promotion.

We also found that when everyone at the IEP meeting is informed on the federal and state guidelines, it reduces the emotional stress on the team. When the guidelines are followed, everyone knows the rules and knows what is expected from everyone else. Parents are not as likely to ask for inappropriate services, and educators are more likely to try to work with the family. In short, it reduces the game-playing. Our own experience has shown that when parents feel they have been misled and manipulated, they become hostile toward the school staff. Developing an atmosphere of trust and respect helps everyone to stay focused on the needs of the student. A personal friend who is a principal makes it a point to sit down with parents who seem defensive and explain the federal guidelines step-by-step. He says it helps take the hostility out of the relationship and the meetings.

What we learned

Our transition from naïve and trusting parents to warrior parents and finally to parent/professionals taught us that we needed to become informed IEP participants. We had been unrealistic in our expectation that the professionals would know how to work with a child like Ryan. We needed their expertise, and they needed ours. By talking with other parents who were willing to share their mistakes and triumphs with us, we learned to become better advocates for our son. Conferences and literature taught us the finer points of Ryan's disability, education, and the law. Graduate school helped to provide us with the educators' perspective. Because of others' willingness to share their experiences, we learned how to be successful advocates for Ryan, and we found it so important to share our own experiences, so others may learn from us as well.

As we worked toward obtaining an appropriate education for Ryan, we began developing skills. We learned how to present our information in an assertive and informed manner. As we continued to do research and look for answers regarding Ryan, we became as informed as many of the educators who sat in the IEP meetings with us. When we felt strongly about an intervention, we continued to present our argument until we obtained the service or support. Together, we became a strong and effective team that advocated successfully for our son.

By attending IEP meetings with other parents, we were both able to hone our skills. Since the meeting was not about Ryan, it was easier to maintain some emotional distance, which enabled us to listen and process the information more effectively. We were developing the skills necessary to hold the school district accountable for how it worked with students with special needs.

When we began working with parents, we were amazed at the numbers of parents who were uninformed about their education rights and the special education process and how easily they could be dissuaded from obtaining what their child needed in school. As a result, we developed a manual, and through workshops we began teaching parents their rights and how the special education process is supposed to work.

By attending graduate school and providing workshops we were able in turn to gain insight into the educators' point of view. We learned that the educators are just as uninformed as the parents. Many have not received training in the IEP process and are not informed on the social ramifications of Asperger Syndrome. Most educators have the student's best interest at heart, but they are unsure of how to help these students to have their educational needs met. The workshops not only helped the educators with the process, they helped both parents and educators to have a glimpse into what issues the others face.

As we made the transition from parents to parent/professionals, we also gained insight into the education system. We learned to make the distinction between the individuals we encountered and the system in which they worked. We met many professionals who were dedicated to working with children and families, and parents who were willing to work with the educators to help them to educate their child. As we both acquired these skills and met these people, we also became more effective advocates for our own son.

What you can do

- Attend meetings with other parents; this will allow you to develop skills for your own child's school meetings without being emotionally involved in the issues.

- Attending meetings with other parents helps to establish parent-to-parent support.

- Do not go into school meetings in a confrontational or aggressive frame of mind. Take the anger out of the situation as much as possible.

- Meet with your child's teacher and principal on a regular basis.

- Do not accept evaluation reports on the day of the meeting. Request that the information be provided and explained several days before the meeting. All the committee's decisions are to be determined on the basis of the information obtained from evaluation, and parents cannot make informed decisions when they are not familiar with the evaluation results.

- If personal or private information is presented to you for the first time at a meeting, immediately stop the meeting. Talk to the professional concerned in private, then determine whether the meeting is to continue or be adjourned for a few days.

- If the meeting is being rushed, request that the meeting should either be slowed down or be adjourned until the school has the time to complete the meeting unrushed.

- Be familiar with the legal guidelines that govern your education system, and make sure your committee follows those guidelines. Do not be afraid to inform them if they are making procedural errors.

- Become familiar with evaluation and how decisions are made from evaluation results; be wary of people who tell you to disregard evaluation results.

- If you do not trust the school district's results from their evaluation, go to an outside source for your child's evaluation.

- Make sure that goals and objectives are observable and measurable, so that you can hold your school district accountable for your child's progress.

- Make sure the education plan that is written is individualized for your child.

Chapter Eight

Filling the Void in Our Community

Isolation

When we lived in the Dallas/Fort Worth Area, we had access to support groups, workshops, and conferences, and we both made use of all these opportunities. We were shocked to find, when we moved to West Texas, that there were very few functioning support groups and even fewer workshops and conferences. In the beginning, DeAnn floundered trying to find a support group for autism. There was one small support group run by a parent/professional who was ready to hand the group to someone else. The group had very few parents, and these parents seemed more interested in complaining than in actually getting assertive and doing something. A school administrator attended every group meeting; she was also our special education coordinator. DeAnn was extremely uncomfortable, so after a couple of meetings she did not return to this group. Another group, for Learning Disabilities, was run by a mother who homeschooled her son and who was very adversarial. The next leader was extremely nice, but the group folded after her death from cancer. DeAnn had presented for this group a few times, but she did not feel that the group addressed our needs. The next group was one for pre-school and young elementary-age children with medical needs. Finally, there was a group for ADHD that came and went several times. It was extremely frustrating to move to an area with no viable support groups, but at this point we were knowledgeable enough to figure things out on our own.

The lack of opportunity to attend workshops was another sacrifice. We live in the largest school district in the area, and the district brings in speakers to present to their staff. During our first year in West Texas, DeAnn naïvely asked the special education director whether parents could attend a presentation by a famous presenter on Inclusion. The director was incensed and informed DeAnn that she did not like having parents and professionals at the same presentation, so the professionals could 'ask their questions.' She did acquiesce and let DeAnn attend that particular presentation, but to our knowledge, DeAnn was the only parent allowed to attend. The special education director continued to have professionals come into her district and present but made sure that if parents were to attend, this would be at a separate presentation. The special education director and some of her staff were always present at these parent presentations.

Our community had an Education Service Center funded through the state that contracted and brought in well-known professionals. The advertising on these was limited, so one had to be well connected with the right person to find out ahead of time who was presenting and when. At one point, a special education director demanded that the Education Service Center not allow parents to attend workshops with the educators. The staff at the Education Service Center told the special education director that parents were always welcome at their workshops. We found it interesting that staff from our school district rarely attended these presentations.

We felt we were far from civilization. DeAnn had to call her parent network long-distance to communicate with her friends.

We had to drive some six hours to go to a conference where everyone was included. DeAnn had grown up in rural Nebraska, but West Texas seemed more isolated than any place we had ever known.

Providing training

For the first year, we tried to keep in contact with the special education director, but we soon came to realize that we were working at cross-purposes, so we moved on from our thinking that we would have a close relationship. The second year, DeAnn tried to start a parent clinic that taught parents their educational rights. Very few parents attended – there seemed to be little interest. The third year, DeAnn managed to convince several agencies to join with her and hold an annual conference on various topics for parents and professionals. This was very successful for several years. Every agency chipped in money or time, whichever they had available, and the Education Service Center paid for the majority of the conference. The group covered a range of topics. At our first conference, we had Kim Peak – the original Rain Man. This was a very successful conference. Our turnout was mostly professional, though a few parents did come. We had a conference on negotiation skills, behavior management, and conflict resolution. After four years, as the group of agencies became smaller and smaller, we stopped organizing the conferences.

Support group

While we were in graduate school, the DSM-IV was released. Shortly afterward, people began asking DeAnn if she would be interested in starting a parent support group for parents of children with Asperger Syndrome. She politely declined, saying that she was in graduate school and did not have the time; she added that maybe after she graduated, she would start one, but she really did not give starting a support group much thought. About a year after she graduated, a professional at an agency asked DeAnn if she still intended to start a support group for AS, and DeAnn answered that she probably would. The agency professional said that part of her job was to set up new support groups, and she would do so for DeAnn. By that afternoon she had set up a place for DeAnn's group to meet and was getting ready to invite people. Knowing that the professional was simply getting DeAnn to do a part of her job and would take credit for her efforts, DeAnn said that she already had a place to meet and she could handle things on her own if she would just begin referring people.

The first support group meeting was to be held at a site called The Cottage at noon, but the office manager had forgotten about the meeting, and the door was locked when DeAnn arrived. DeAnn's friend from the Education Service Center, two other mothers, and DeAnn sat on a blanket in front of The Cottage and had a picnic lunch. Shortly afterward, the local newspaper ran an article on our support group, and a new mother showed up the following month. She said that the article reminded her a lot of her sixteen-year-old son. The more she described her son, the more convinced DeAnn was that she needed to have him assessed to rule out autism. She suggested that the mother take her son to the psychologist in Houston who had diagnosed Ryan with Asperger Syndrome. When the mother came back with her evaluation report, her son had been diagnosed with autism. She has attended almost every meeting since and is now on the executive committee.

For the first year, DeAnn wanted the group to be composed of parents supporting each other, but very few people attended. The second year, DeAnn began inviting professionals to come and speak on various topics, such as language pragmatics, education law, and evaluation. We listed our meetings and topics in the paper, and more and more people began to attend. For a short time, someone who worked with the school system attended the meetings, and this made some of the parents extremely uncomfortable. By the third year, parents asked if we could alternate professional meetings and parent meetings, and if at the parent meetings we could invite only parents. Having talked with other support group leaders, DeAnn found that this alternating between professional groups and parent groups is considered the most effective method. At each monthly meeting the support group has had at least one new participant, and the group continues to grow.

Social skills group

When we had moved to West Texas in 1993, we found that by their own report the local professionals we encountered knew relatively little about Asperger Syndrome or autism. Over the years, we began hearing that these same professionals had formed themselves into a small group, and they referred to themselves as the 'autism team.' We were cautious about their level of knowledge. What concerned us was that not only were these the same professionals whom local and surrounding school districts used for staff development and parent training on these topics, they were also the professionals who ran the social skills groups for our school district.

When Ryan started the seventh grade, DeAnn began looking for a social skills group outside what the school district had to offer. The groups she found were unimpressive. One was run by a counselor who had no training in Asperger Syndrome. Her groups consisted of children with behavior problems. Matt later learned that her groups could be as large as 14 to 20 students to two adults – a size that was much too large to be effective. Another group was also run by an individual who had no training in Asperger

Syndrome. This social skills group focused on self-esteem. We both felt that Ryan would not benefit from any existing group in our area, so we did not pursue the matter further.

After our visit to Yale Child Study Center, we realized that we had to find a social skills group for Ryan, though we still could not locate one we thought was even adequate. After some thought, we decided that together we would run our own group. We both had graduate degrees, DeAnn in special education, Matt in counseling. DeAnn began to email and call people. She asked about research and to whom she could talk. She discovered that there is in fact very little research, but a handful of people have started their own social skills groups. DeAnn spent a summer doing research and talking with others who ran social skills groups, and she ordered any book she could find that addressed social skills. By early fall, she had contacted several families of children with Learning Disabilities, Attention Deficit Disorder, High Functioning Autism, and Asperger Syndrome. In September, we began our group. In January, Ryan's speech therapist began working with our group. Her expertise in speech helped us to refine our social skills group even further. We found that the best group size was six students at a time, with two to three adults present.

Our research and experience from the social skills group taught us that we were already doing quite a bit of work with Ryan's social skills without realizing it. Games, movies, and books can be used as tools to promote reciprocity and reading body language. Community excursions can be turned into an arena of determining whether the child is generalizing the skills obtained from speech therapy and the home lessons. Grocery stores and restaurants are a gold mine for practicing manners and good social skills. Even working with animals can be a lesson on how animals and people talk with their bodies. In short, many parents are very capable of working with their child in developing social skills.

If a parent does decide to enroll their child in a social skills group, we recommend that they watch for several characteristics. The group should be small – in our experience no more than eight students at a time – and it should present structured lessons. While self-esteem is an admirable skill to develop, the social skills group should be working primarily on skills such as listening, beginning conversations, watching body language, and so on. A mix of student issues is a very good quality: the group should not consist of just Asperger Syndrome or high functioning autism, but should include other types of disorders that have social issues, such as Attention Deficit Disorder, Learning Disabilities, speech disabilities, and so on. The group leaders should make themselves available to work with the parents on how to expand the learned skills into the community.

The conference

In December 1999 DeAnn and another parent flew to El Paso to talk to a parent support group that had successfully sponsored a conference. They had enlisted the help of their local Education Service Center, and eight hundred people had attended their first event. Feeling that their support group could be as successful with a conference, DeAnn and the parent got a small group of parents together and compared stories. They discovered that all the parents were struggling with finding local professionals informed on Asperger Syndrome and autism. After comparing notes, the parents found that many of the teachers and administrators did not have the budget or the time to go to Dallas and Houston for conferences. The group voted to bring the speakers to the community to train our educators.

The support group decided to invite Dr. Tony Attwood, an expert on autism spectrum disorders, and Dr. Temple Grandin, an adult with autisn who is also an expert on livestock behavior and facility design, to present. DeAnn contacted Dr. Attwood, who said he would come. When he told DeAnn the cost of his honorarium, she knew that the group had to start some fundraising to cover the speakers' expenses. Dr. Temple Grandin also agreed to come, provided the group could also arrange a speaking engagement on her own subject – cattle. She suggested DeAnn call the local university's animal science department. It took a little while to muster the courage to call the university and explain the correlation between autism and cattle, but when DeAnn did so the university was happy to accommodate the group. After quite a lengthy correspondence between Dr. Attwood, Dr. Grandin, and DeAnn, they finally came up with a day for the conference.

The small support group met with the director for the Education Service Center to enlist their help with registration, the printing of brochures, and the publicity to the schools, explaining that we did not want to ask for money from the Education Service Center – we wanted to raise that on our own. The director, a long-time supporter of parents' efforts in the community, agreed to help us with the conference.

The next step was raising the necessary money. The support group organized several fund-raisers, while DeAnn began writing for grants. She had previously been unsuccessful in applying for grants, so this time she called up the foundations and talked to a key person ahead of time about completing the proposals, explaining that we were a new support group, and that this was our first big project. DeAnn submitted her proposals, and we waited for the response.

One grant that was submitted to a state agency was proposed to cover parent stipends for the conference. DeAnn had a friend who sat on the board. Our goal was to have 800 participants at our conference. This particular grant would not cover more that 49 percent of the total budget for the conference. The grant committee had our friend call during a break in their meeting. They did not feel that a local group in West Texas could raise more than the 51 percent required, or have 800 conference participants, so they wanted to know how much we had raised so far. When DeAnn told her how much we had raised, her friend started laughing – we had far exceeded our 51 percent. The support group was awarded the grant, and 100 parents and others were able to attend the conference free of charge.

We enlisted as much help as we could find. The local visitors' bureau provided the presenters' gifts and nametags for audience participants. We enlisted support through gifts in kind through the local school district, the PTI, local shops and grocery stores. One couple volunteered to get Continuing Education Units (CEUs), these are for professionals who needed to receive class credit to retain their licence or certification. Another parent spent two weeks before the conference calling newspapers in the surrounding communities to advertise our conference through articles.

Two weeks before the conference, our registration numbers hovered at 400; by the time the day of the conference came, we had close to 800 participants. They came primarily from our immediate surrounding communities, including from New Mexico. The conference evaluations came back with glowing reports. The first local annual Asperger Syndrome/autism conference had been a success. We are currently planning next year's conference.

At a subsequent meeting, a leader from the school district's 'autism team' said, 'It is good that you brought these big-name speakers to the community, but do not forget that there are local professionals who are just as good.' DeAnn apologized to him if we had given the impression of ignoring the local professionals. She explained that so far there was only a small group of individuals available to work with school personnel. As he was aware, this small group of people could barely keep up with their workload at their own districts, much less be available for the rural communities. Our goal was to reach as many educators and professionals as we could, so that they would be able to develop skills to work with their own students without having to rely on a handful of professionals. Several people in the room were administrators from the rural areas; they nodded their heads as DeAnn spoke. The autism team leader conceded her point.

When we first moved to West Texas, we were surprised at the lack of parent support systems and training there. We were fortunate to find other families who were also concerned about this lack of support and information; we banded together, found community support, and managed to fill the void in our region.

What we learned

We learned not to expect the professionals to provide the necessary supports and interventions in the community, and to be wary of those who presented themselves as experts in autism or Asperger Syndrome. We were amazed at the lack of knowledgeable professionals in our community.

We identified three areas of support that we felt were missing in our community: (1) support groups; (2) social skills groups; (3) informed professionals. The support group was formed to help parents meet other parents and to become informed on professionals in our local community who could help them. The social skills group was formed as a direct result of not being able to locate a professional who, we felt, was able to lead a group for adolescents with Asperger Syndrome and related disorders. The final area of concern was the lack of informed professionals, and all the parents in the support group complained about this. As a result, we all decided to sponsor a conference to help members in the community to gain information and insight into the world of Asperger Syndrome and autism. The conference was a success.

In the process of conducting the support group, the social skills group, and the conference, we discovered that we had stepped on some local professionals' toes. They seemed to feel disregarded. This was certainly not our aim. We learned that regardless of one's good intentions, sometimes feelings get hurt.

What you can do

- Look for a support group that supports your needs.
- If you cannot find a support group that you are comfortable with, start up your own.
- Ask your school district or a local agency to help support your group's efforts.
- If your community does not have a particular support (e.g., social skills group), consider starting one yourself.
- If your child's school personnel cannot attend conferences outside your local community, consider sponsoring a local conference. Many support groups are able to do so with the help of an agency, local school district, or local education center.

Starting a support group

- Be patient – forming a group takes lots of time and organization.
- Do not try to do it all by yourself. Ask for volunteers.
- Find financial help for copies, postage, and so forth.
- Get your group listed in the community pages of your local newspaper; it is generally free.

- Ask your local newspaper to run an article on your group.

- Be aware that you cannot please everyone. Some parents will not like the way you run your group, others may not enjoy participating in support groups.

- Charge some type of dues; people generally value services and products they have had to pay for.

- Ask local professionals to present to your group – most will be happy to do so.

- Alternate two different types of groups: one with professionals presenting, the other for parents only.

- Be aware that if you provide childcare, liability can be an issue. We met at lunchtime and made the parents responsible for watching their own children in order to avoid the issue.

- Obtain both Officers and Directors Insurance and General Liability Insurance for your group.

- As much as possible, meet on the same day, at the same time, and in the same place.

- Check with legal counsel on your fiduciary responsibility when you begin obtaining donations and moneys from fundraising.

Becoming your child's social skills coach

- Watch peer interaction and determine where it is breaking down for your child.

- Watch your child's social behavior.

- Watch other children. Determine if they are 'nurturers' or 'predators.'

- Identify any 'sensory' issues that interfere with your child's social interactions.

- Watch for 'teachable moments.'

- Explain by intellectualizing social encounters for your child.

- Try to anticipate social encounters and explain to your child beforehand what will happen, what you expect him/her to do, and what options your child will have during the encounter.

- After the encounter, debrief your child on what was good and what needs to be worked on.

- Keep a journal of your child's interactions.

- Sports can be a wonderful avenue to develop social skills and motor coordination:
  ○ Games can develop reciprocity, sharing, and joint attention.
  ○ Be cautious of certain team sports, (such as soccer or basketball) which may require too much social interaction for your child.
  ○ Look for sports where the focus is more on the individual rather than the team (such as swimming, tae kwon do, horseback riding).

Assessing a social skills group: what to look for

- Small group size – no more than eight students.

- Age range close to your child's own age.

- Students with a variety of issues, such as ADHD, LD, and typical kids.

- Works on social issues like starting a conversation, watching body language, and so on.

- Meets regularly.
- Meets for at least 45 minutes.
- Students have fun.

Chapter Nine

Preparing for the Future

Being involved

Several well-meaning friends have told us that we have devoted far too much time working towards getting Ryan's social and academic needs met, and that we should not be so involved in his schooling. We both know a few educators who feel the same way, but we totally disagree. Early on, we realized that it was necessary for us to invest time and energy in learning the education system to ensure that Ryan was prepared to enter the adult world. It is frightening to think what would have happened to him if we had not continued to be active participants in his education. We have both heard stories from other parents who did not realize until several years had passed that their child had not received interventions that might have helped with academics or enhanced their social skills. Many children with Asperger Syndrome are not identified correctly until they are in their teens. The severity of their impairment may not be fully appreciated, because they have demonstrated the ability to satisfy the academic requirements and display acceptable classroom behavior. The problem is that socially these children are behind, and they get further behind as time goes on if they do not receive the necessary social skills training.

It is important to state that while we have had to deal with some difficult people in our efforts to secure supports and services for Ryan, they were in the minority. On the whole, the professionals were helpful and supportive in our efforts to satisfy Ryan's educational needs. In the portfolio that DeAnn developed for Ryan, almost every teacher wrote that they had enjoyed working with Ryan and had learned a lot from him. Ryan was fortunate that he did not have a bad teacher while he was in public school. The problems we encountered were not due to the individuals who worked with us – they were a reflection of the system. It is also important to state that it was the difficult people who increased our resolve and gave us the motivation to continue to pursue what we believed were appropriate and needed services for Ryan. Anger and frustration can be very effective motivators when you are pushing for services that the school district does not consider appropriate to the needs of your child. Federal and state laws are in place today because parents were unhappy with the existing system. It is when parents stay in the anger mode too long that it becomes counterproductive.

We have seen the consequences of parents not getting involved in their child's education. As an employee of a local agency, one of Matt's duties was to advocate educationally for his school-age clients. Parents had a tendency to rely too heavily on his assistance, without taking steps toward becoming self-reliant. Agency employees tend to have a large caseload and are therefore limited in the time they have to work with individual clients. Additionally, the agency employees are not trained on specific disabilities or the IEP process. As a result, agency employment turnover rates are high due to frustration and employee burnout, and the client's needs are often not met. This is the primary problem with parents leaving it up to others to see to it that their child's educational needs are being satisfied.

Parents of children receiving special education services in public school are in a unique position, because they have been given the right, by law, to be involved in all decisions concerning their child's education. Along with this right comes the responsibility to become informed, participating members of their child's IEP committee. Instead of leaving it up to the educators to carry the entire burden of teaching their child, as we did in the beginning, parents need to participate as much as they are able. We well know from our years of experience that there is a great deal to learn. When parents accept their responsibility as members of the IEP team and understand that when they participate – even if it is just asking questions to get clarification – their child will have a better chance of receiving what he or she needs. We believe this to be the case based on numerous conversations with educators who have the idea that many parents do not care about their child's education, especially when they do not show up for IEP meetings. When we have had these discussions, we routinely bring up the fact that it is our belief that parents do indeed care, but they believe that educating their child is the responsibility of the school system. The special education process is overwhelming, and both of us certainly found this to be the case in the early years.

As a Licensed Professional Counselor in private practice, Matt also has worked with families of children diagnosed with a disability. In addition to counseling, Matt helps them to develop effective strategies for working with the education system. The impact of the education system on the family unit is surprisingly consistent: many families of children who receive special education services have experienced many of the same difficulties that we have. The stress of not only parenting a child with a disability but also finding the necessary support, working with agencies, and getting the appropriate services through the education system contributes to family tension. Although we do not have the actual statistics, we are aware that the divorce rate among families of children with disabilities is higher than the national average; we have had several friends whose marriages did not last, due to the strain.

DeAnn has received phone calls from parents who realized quite late that there were serious problems with the way the school had been working with their child. By the time a student is in high school, it is very difficult to get the support they need, because there is so little time to get interventions in place so close to graduation. Many parents want a quick fix, or they want someone else to take care of their child's school problems. Some parents have called DeAnn while their child was still in elementary school. Only a few of them were willing to put in the time necessary to learn how to advocate effectively for their child. A big difference can be found in the level of functioning of children whose parents advocated early on, as opposed to those who did not. In most cases, the parents who waited were those who put their faith and trust in the school system or the agency system. It is sad to say that this was misguided, but we found it to be true in our own case as well as in others'. We learned early on that it was unrealistic to expect the school system or the agency system to know how to work effectively with our son without our participation.

We are just beginning to realize the impact that Asperger Syndrome has had on our extended families. We have recently learned that other members were struggling with Ryan's diagnosis, and they also needed support that we were unable to provide. Some wanted to help, but did not know how; others did not understand and therefore accept that sometimes discipline issues needed to be addressed differently with Ryan, and they expressed frustration with the fact that we would not allow them to discipline Ryan when he was younger. Some family members still do not understand the impact AS has on how Ryan interacts with the world, leading to conflicts between them and us. Our hope for the future is that interested family members will come forward to offer their friendship to Ryan. He is a young man who desperately needs the support of his extended family in his transition to being successful in the adult world.

An unexpected impact of Ryan's Asperger's Syndrome is the realization that he is not the only family member with the syndrome. Though neither one of us is qualified to diagnose Asperger Syndrome, we know the characteristics well enough to recognize them in family members on both sides of our family. On occasion we have discussed the unusual behaviors of these family members, but our comments are only just now being taken seriously by a few of our relatives.

Secondary education

We are constantly aware of the need to prepare Ryan for his adult life. We feel that we started preparing Ryan for adulthood when we began advocating for his education, and for years, just like other parents, we have worked on building independence through household chores: cooking, doing dishes, laundry, dusting, vacuuming, and so on. In stores and restaurants, we have worked with Ryan on things like counting his change and showing good manners. Generally, we have helped Ryan to develop adult living skills just as parents do with typical children.

When DeAnn presented to a class of graduate students at the local public university on parent issues, the professor, who has been a good friend of hers for several years, asked her what her greatest concern was for Ryan. DeAnn replied that our greatest concern is for Ryan to find someone who will become his life-long companion. It is our hope that whoever she is, she will be good to Ryan. She added that we feel that this is a concern of every parent.

It is important for us to say that Ryan is a great kid. We love him very much, we are very proud of him, and we feel blessed that he is our son. He has made so much progress over the years. He has a pleasant personality, one that adults are drawn to, and we feel that he has the potential to develop into a successful adult. He recently asked DeAnn, 'Mom, what is it that makes me special?' DeAnn responded, 'You are special because you bring out the good in other people.' Ryan beamed with pride.

When Ryan was initially diagnosed, we were not given much hope for his future. We began the education process like any other parents, relying completely on the expertise of the educators, believing they knew what to do. We found that it was unrealistic to expect them to have all the answers. We were motivated to become involved in Ryan's education because it was obvious that the educators did not know how to work with a child like him. As we became more knowledgeable about interventions for Ryan, we encountered resistance from the educators and this, in turn, motivated us to develop skills on negotiation and special education law. We found that we needed to accept responsibility for ensuring that Ryan received an appropriate education, which he is guaranteed under federal and state laws. Our experiences helped us become informed, participating members of Ryan's IEP team.

It was the incident at school when Ryan was thought to be following a girl that moved us to decide that we would probably homeschool Ryan after ninth grade. After much research on homeschooling, we determined that we could provide Ryan with an academic program that would prepare him for college. More importantly, between us we could provide him with more social opportunities in controlled environments that would allow us to monitor him and provide feedback on his progress. When we were at Yale Child Study Center, Dr. Ami Klin had told us that Ryan had only a small window of opportunity to develop social skills, whereas he had a lifetime to develop his academic skills. After considering where Ryan was at that point academically and socially, we decided that we could not afford for him to continue in public school. We were also persuaded to homeschool Ryan because of the experiences of DeAnn's brother in high school. He had been teased mercilessly, and this seemed to be happening more to Ryan. We are confident that his teachers did put a stop to this behavior whenever they became aware of it, but in a high school there are just too many opportunities for teasing and bullying unnoticed by teachers and staff. Ryan has high self-esteem, and we wish for this to continue. In any case, we are interested in Ryan learning to behave like a typical adult, not a typical high school student.

DeAnn made the IEP committee aware of our intention to homeschool Ryan at his IEP meeting at the end of ninth grade. Since it would be Ryan's last IEP meeting, DeAnn felt comfortable attending without Matt. The committee members and the special education director were obviously upset about our decision and tried to persuade DeAnn to change her mind, but DeAnn held firm. She announced that we would start homeschooling during the summer. We realized that when we started homeschooling, we would be closing a chapter of our lives.

Homeschooling

As part of the transition into homeschooling, Ryan and DeAnn began taking Scottish Country Dance Lessons. DeAnn thought it sounded like fun, and since we have Scottish ancestry on both sides of our family, we agreed that it would be nice to expose Ryan to his heritage. After a few lessons it became evident that it would take a lot of practice for Ryan to learn the steps – we had no idea that it would be so difficult to learn the dances. This did not discourage us, because the benefits of dancing and the social opportunities would make the experience worthwhile. Several boys of Ryan's age showed up for the dance lesson in the fifth week of class. After an hour of dancing, the dancers have their first break. Many parents of children on the autism spectrum approach unstructured time with a sense of dread, and we are no different, because this is when it tends to fall apart for these kids. Sometimes the others realize that something is different about Ryan and avoid him. Occasionally a child will approach Ryan and attempt to engage him. Usually we watch helplessly as the social encounter deteriorates and the other child drifts away from Ryan. It is painful beyond words to see the hurt look on his face. He knows he has done something wrong, but he does not know what. This time, a boy sat down on the sofa next to Ryan and began talking to him. The boy did not appear to be put off by Ryan in the least. This was a first.

At the end of the dance lessons, another boy walked up to Ryan and gave him his phone number and email address. He invited Ryan to the skating rink later that afternoon. This boy offered to pick Ryan up (he had just learned to drive) and take him to the rink. Although it was a nice gesture, DeAnn declined. He also told Ryan about bowling, skating, and a youth group that Ryan could join. Several homeschooling moms came up to DeAnn and congratulated her on our decision to homeschool Ryan, and they offered their support. They also told DeAnn how much more accepting homeschooled children are of kids that are different. Skeptical at that point, DeAnn smiled, thinking, 'I've heard this before. I've been disappointed too many times to get my hopes up.' Encouraged nonetheless, DeAnn came home and told Matt about how things had gone.

A couple of hours later Ryan and DeAnn went to the skating rink. Fortunately, Ryan was familiar with this rink; he had skated there several times when he was in elementary school. The difference this time was that the rink was reserved for a few hours by the Homeschooling Association. They arrived a little late on purpose, because these are not the best situations for Ryan. DeAnn could handle one hour of torture watching Ryan being excluded, but not two hours. Ryan is a very bad skater, on top of it all. We had both tried to teach him how to skate, as had the occupational therapist. In addition, the kids at the roller-skating rink had always been rowdy, and DeAnn feared that with his coordination problems, Ryan was going to get hurt. Just being here was a leap of faith. The boy who invited Ryan walked up to him and said, 'Come on, Ryan, sit with us.' Off Ryan went, to sit down with some teenagers he had never met before. There were a couple of very attractive girls close to Ryan's age in the group. DeAnn had brought her laptop and a book, so she could pretend that she wasn't watching Ryan. She could see out of the corner of her eye that Ryan was blushing with excitement. They were talking to him. It was obvious that the group accepted Ryan. Soon the six teenagers got up and went to the floor to skate. DeAnn's heart sank. She tried not to watch. She saw the group skating, and one boy far behind the group. DeAnn cringed inside. She just knew it was Ryan – but when she looked closer, she realized it wasn't. It took a few seconds to spot Ryan, because he was in the middle of the group...skating. His skating was awkward and slow, but the group continued to surround him, going at his pace. Soon they all stopped next to the tables, close to where DeAnn was sitting. They introduced Ryan to another mom. They stayed there for several minutes, involving Ryan in their conversations, which included a great deal of laughter. Soon it was time for the kids to leave. A boy whom Ryan had met at the rink stayed behind to work with Ryan on his skating. DeAnn was amazed at how much better Ryan could skate after only thirty minutes of instruction by this accommodating young man. As they left the building, three boys in a pickup truck called out, 'Bye, Ryan.' And then they waved.

When we think back over the past sixteen years, we have to conclude that this was the first time that either of us had ever seen Ryan so included in a group. The teenagers had no idea what they had done for Ryan and for us. DeAnn was amazed at how naturally it had occurred. No one had gone in ahead of time to train staff, quoting the law and bringing articles on Asperger Syndrome. No IEP goals and objectives had been written. There was not a therapist in sight. No adults instructed these teenagers to include Ryan, or even how to include him. No one came in and taught these teenagers about accepting differences, Inclusion, and Asperger Syndrome, and yet there Ryan was sitting and talking with a group of perfect strangers, save one. Ryan had looked so relaxed and typical. Perhaps the world will be kinder to Ryan than we expected. It is a new beginning, and Ryan's future looks bright.

References

Asperger's Disorder, Autism, and Nonverbal Learning Disabilities

Attwood, A. (1998) *Asperger's Syndrome: A Guide for Parents and Professionals.* London: Jessica Kingsley Publishers.

Bauer, S. (2000) *Asperger Syndrome* [Internet]. Available: www.udel.edu/bkirby/asperger/

Cohen, S. (1998) *Targeting Autism: What We Know, Don't Know, and We Can Do to Help Young Children with Autism and Related Disorders.* Los Angeles, CA: University of California Press.

Frith, U. (ed.) (1991) *Autism and Asperger Syndrome.* London: Cambridge University Press.

Fullerton, A., Stratton, J., Coyne, P. and Gray, C. (1996) *Higher Functioning Adolescents and Young Adults with Autism: A Teacher's Guide.* Austin, TX: Pro-ed.

Klin, A. (1994) 'Asperger syndrome.' *Psychoses and Pervasive Developmental Disorders, 3,*1, 131–148.

Klin, A. and Volkmar, F. R. (1995) *Asperger syndrome: Some Guidelines for Assessment, Diagnosis, and Intervention.* [Internet]. Available: info.med.Yale.edu...stdy/autism/Idabro2.html

Klin, A. and Volkmar, F. R. (1995) *Asperger Syndrome: Some Guidelines for Parents.* [Internet]. Available: info.med.Yale.edu...stdy/autism/Idabro2.html

Klin, A., Volkmar, F. R. and Sparrow, S. S. (eds) (2000) *Asperger Syndrome.* New York: Guilford Press.

Kohn, A. (1993) *Punished by Rewards: The Trouble with Gold Stars, Incentive Plans, A's, Praise and Other Bribes.* New York: Houghton Mifflin Company.

Rourke, B. P. (1995) 'Asperger syndrome.' In A. Klin, S. S. Sparrow, F. R. Volkmar, D. V. Cicchetti and B. P. Rourke (eds) *Syndrome of Nonverbal Learning Disabilities: Neurodevelopmental Manifestations* pp. 93–118 New York: Guilford Press.

Schopler, E. and Mesibov, G. B. (1992) *High-Functioning Individuals with Autism.* New York: Plenum Press.

Smith-Myles, B. and Simpson, R. L. (1998) *Asperger Syndrome: A Guide for Educators and Parents.* Austin, TX: Pro-Ed.

Tanguay, P. B. (2001) *Nonverbal Learning Disabilities at Home: A Parent's Guide.* London: Jessica Kingsley Publishers.

Tanguay, P. B. (2002) *Nonverbal Learning Disabilities at School: Educating Students with NLD, Asperger Syndrome and Related Conditions.* London: Jessica Kingsley Publishers.

Thompson, S. (1997) *The Source for Nonverbal Learning Disabilities.* East Moline, IL: LinguiSystems.

Developing social skills

Aarons, J. and Gittens, T. (1998) *Autism: A Social Skills Approach for Children and Adolescents.* Bicester, Oxon, UK: Winslow Press Limited.

Begun, R. W. (ed.) (1995) *Ready to Use Social Skills Lessons and Activities.* West Nyack, NY: The Center for Applied Research in Education.

Duke, M. P., Nowicki, S. and Martin, E. (1996) *Teaching Your Child the Language of Social Success.* Atlanta, GA: Peachtree Publishers Ltd.

Frankel, F. (1996) *Good Friends Are Hard to Find: Help Your Child Find, Make and Keep Friends.* Los Angeles, CA: Perspective Publishing.

Freeman, S. and Dake, L. (1997) *Teach Me Language: A Language Manual for Children with Autism, Asperger's Syndrome and Related Developmental Disorders.* Langley, BC: SKF Books.

Howlin, P., Baron-Cohen, S. and Hadwin, J. (1999) *Teaching Children with Autism to Mind-Read: A Practical Guide.* New York: John Wiley and Sons.

Matthews, A. (1991) *Making Friends: A Guide to Getting Along with People.* New York: Price Stern Sloan, Inc.

McGann, W. and Werven, G. (1999) *Social Communication Skills for Children: A Workbook for Principle Centered Communication.* Austin, TX: Pro-ed.

Nowicki, S. and Duke, M. P. (1992) *Helping the Child who Doesn't Fit In.* Atlanta, GA: Peachtree Publishers Ltd.

Packer, A. J. (1997) *How Rude! The Teenagers' Guide to Good Manners, Proper Behavior, and Not Grossing People Out.* Minneapolis, MN: Free Spirit Publishing.

Quill, K. A. (1995) *Teaching Children with Autism: Strategies to Enhance Communication and Socialization.* Detroit, MI: Delmar Publishers Inc.

Sheridan, S. M. (1998) *Why Don't They Like Me?: Helping Your Child Make and Keep Friends.* Longmont, CO: Sopris West.

Winner, M. G. (2000) *Inside Out: What Makes a Person With Social Cognitive Deficits Tick?* San Jose, CA: Michelle Garcia Winner, SLP.

Advocating and negotiating

Anderson, W., Chitwood, S. and Hayden, D. (1990) *Negotiating the Special Education Maze,* 2nd edn. Rockville, MD: Woodbine House.

Bateman, B. D. and Linden, M. A. (1998) *Better IEPs: How to Develop Legally Correct and Educationally Useful Programs,* 3rd edn. Longmont, CO: Sopris West.

Cutler, B. C. (1993) *You, Your Child and Special Education: A Guide to Making the System Work.* Baltimore, MD: Paul H. Brookes Publishing Co.

Des Jardins, C. (ed.) (1993) *How to Get Services by Being Assertive.* Chicago, IL: Family Resource Center on Disabilities.

Fisher, R. and Brown, S. (1988) *Getting Together: Building Relationships as We Negotiate.* New York: Penguin Books.

Fisher, R., Ury, W. and Patton, B. (1991) *Getting to Yes: Negotiating Agreement without Giving In,* 2nd edn. New York: Penguin Books.

Ury, W. (1993) *Getting Past No: Negotiating Your Way from Confrontation to Cooperation.* New York: Bantam Book.

Wright, P. W. D. and Wright, P. D. (1999) *Wrightslaw: Special Education Law.* Hartford, CT: Harbor House Law Press.

Anecdotal stories on Asperger's Syndrome and autism

Barron, J. and Barron, S. (1992) *There's a Boy in Here.* New York: Avon.

Fling, E. (2000) *Eating an Artichoke: A Mother's Perspective on Asperger Syndrome.* London: Jessica Kingsley Publishers.

Gerlach, E. K. (1999) *Just This Side of Normal: Glimpses into Life with Autism.* Eugene, OR: Four Leaf Press.

Grandin, T. and Scariano, M. (1991) *Emergence: Labeled Autistic.* Novato, CA: Arena Press.

Grandin, T. (1995) *Thinking in Pictures and Other Reports from My Life with Autism.* New York: Vintage Books.

Hart, C. (1989) *Without Reason: A Family Copes with Two Generations of Autism.* Arlington, TX: Future Horizons.

McDonell, J. T. (1993) *News from the Border: A Mother's Memoir of her Autistic Son.* New York: Ticknor and Fields.

Willey, L. H. (1999) *Pretending to Be Normal: Living with Asperger's Syndrome.* London: Jessica Kingsley Publishers.

Willey, L. H. (2001) *Asperger Syndrome in the Family: Redefining Normal.* London: Jessica Kingsley Publishers.

Miscellaneous

Wilens, T. E. (1999) *Straight Talk about Psychiatric Medications for Kids.* New York: Guilford Press.

Wodrich, D. L. (1997) *A Guide for Nonpsychologists: Children's Psychological Testing,* 3rd edn. Baltimore, MD: Paul H. Brookes Publishing company

Newsletters, Publications, and Websites

AA News. Asperger's Association of New England, 1301 Centre Street, Newton Centre, MA 02459;
E-mail: info@aane.org
www.aane.org

Action for ASD. Pleasant View Farm, Goodshawfold, Rossendale, Lancashire BB4 8UF;
E-mail: info@actionasd.org
www.actionasd.org.uk

The Advocate. The Autism Society of America, 7910 Woodmont Avenue, Suite 300, Bethesda, MD 20814-3067;
E-mail: action_alert@autism.org
www.autism-society.org

The ARC. The Arc of the United States, 1010 Wayne Avenue, Suite 650, Silver Spring, MD 20910;
E-mail: info@thearc.org
www.thearc.org

Autism Asperger's Digest. Future Horizons, Inc., 721 West Abram Street, Arlington, TX 76013 (800) 486-0727;
Email: edfuture@onramp.net
www.futurehorizons-autism.com

Autism Research Review International. Autism Research Institute, 4182 Adams Avenue, San Diego, CA 92116;
www.autism.com/ari

Beach Center on Families and Disability. The University of Kansas Haworth Hall, Room 3136, 1200 Sunnyside Avenue, Lawrence, KS 66045-7537;
E-mail: beach@dole.Isi.ukans.edu
www.Isi.ukans.edu/beach

Center for the Study of Autism. PO Box 4538, Salem, OR 97302;
www.autism.org

Connections Newsletter. Gustein, Sheely and Associates, P.C., 1177 West Loop South, Suite 530, Houston, TX 77027;
www.connectionscenter.com

Cure Autism Now. 5455 Wilshire Blvd., Suite 715, Los Angeles, CA 90036;
www.canfoundation.org

Disability Solutions. 9220 SW Barbur Blvd., #119–179, Portland, OR, 97219-5428;
E-mail: subscription@disabilitysolutions.org
www.disabilitysolutions.org

Division TEACCH. CB#7180; 310 Medical School Wing E, The University of North Carolina at Chapel Hill, Chapel Hill, NC 27599-7180;
E-mail: teacch@unc.edu
www.unc.edu/depts/teacch

Exceptional Parent. Psy-Ed Corp., 555 Kinderkamack Road, Oradell, NJ 07649-1517;
E-mail: webmaster@eparent.com
www.eparent.com

Families for Early Autism Treatment (FEAT). PO Box 255722, Sacramento, CA 95865-5722.
www.FEAT.org

Future Horizons. 721 W. Abram At., Arlington, TX 76013
www.Future-Horizons-autism.com

The Gray Center. P.O. Box 67, Jenison, MI 49429;
www.thegraycenter.org

Journal of Autism and Developmental Disorders. Kluwer
Academic/Plenum Publishers, 233 Spring Street, New York, NY
10013-1522;
E-mail: services@wkap.nl
www.wkap.nl/journalhome/htm/0162-3257

Learning Disabilities Association of America (LDA).
4156 Library Road, Pittsburgh, PA 15234-1349;
E-mail: Idanatl@ usaor.net
www.Idanatl.org

Looking Up: The Monthly International Autism Newsletter.
PO Box 25727, London, SW19 1WF, England; Tel: 1815427702;
(0) 20-8542-7702
E-mail: info@lookingupautism.org
www.lookingupautism.org

MAAP Newsletter. More Able Autistic Persons, Inc., PO Box 524,
Crown Point, IN 46307;
E-mail: chart@netnitco.net
www.netnitco.net/users/chart/maap.html

The Morning News. Jenison Public School, editor: Carol Gray, 2140
Bauer Road, Jenison, MI 49428;

Narrative. National Alliance for Autism Research, 414 Wall Street,
Research Park, Princeton, NJ 08540; Tel: (609) 430-9160; (888)
777-NAAR;
E-mail: vick-ih@artsci.net
www.babydoc.home.pipeline.com/naar/naar.html

National Information Clearinghouse for Children and Youth with Disabilities (NICHCY). PO Box 1492, Washington, DC 20013;
E-mail: nichcy@aed.org
www.nichcy.org

NLD on the Web.
www.nldontheweb.org

Pacesetter Newsletter. Parent Advocacy Coalition for Educational Rights (PACER), 8161 Normandale Boulevard, Minneapolis, MN 55317;
E-mail: webmaster@pacer.org
www.pacer.org

PDD NETWORK Newsletter. PDD/Asperger's Support Group;
E-mail: BHULT40@aol.com
www.PDDAspergerSupportCT.org

The Source. Asperger Syndrome Coalition for the United States., PO Box 2577 Jacksonville, FL 32203-2577;
www.asperger.org

TASH (formerly known as The Association for Persons with Severe Handicaps)
29 W. Susquehanna Avenue, Suite 210, Baltimore, MD 21204;
E-mail: nweiss@tash.org
www.tash.org

Yale-LDA Social Learning Disabilities Project. 230 South Frontage Road, New Haven, CT 06520-7900;
www.info.med.yale.edu/chldstudy/autism

Internet Resources

Americans with Disabilities Act Document Center.
www.janweb.icdi.wvu.edu/kinder/index.htm

Asperger's Disorder Homepage.
www.ummed.edu/pub/o/ozbayrak/asperger.html

Dr. Tony Attwood.
www.tonyattwood.com

Autism Network International.
www.ani.ac

Autism Resources.
www.autism-info.com

BehaveNet(r).
www.behavenet.com

Disability Resources Monthly.
www.disabilityresources.org

Family Village: A Global Community of Disability-Related Resources.
www.familyvillage.wisc.edu/index.htmlx

National Institutes of Mental Health (NIMH).
www.nimh.nih.gov/publicat/autism.cfm

Online Asperger Syndrome Information and Support (OASIS).
www.udel/edu/bkirby/asperger

raain (Reaching Aspergers/Autism through Information and Networking).
www.raain.org

Special Child.
www.specialchild.com

Index